Power in the Roll

Power in the Roll

A Life at Full Throttle
After Spinal Cord Injury

JESI STRACHAM

Foreword by AMBER BALCAEN

Toplight

Jefferson, North Carolina

Unless otherwise noted,
all photographs are from the author's collection

ISBN (print) 978-1-4766-9851-9
ISBN (ebook) 978-1-4766-5633-5

LIBRARY OF CONGRESS CATALOGING-IN-PUBLICATION DATA

Library of Congress Control Number 2025031024

Front cover image and design by Catawba Creative.

Printed in the United States of America

Toplight is an imprint of McFarland & Company, Inc., Publishers

Toplight

*Box 611, Jefferson, North Carolina 28640
www.toplightbooks.com*

To pre-injury Jesi, I wish I had known
how to help you sooner.
Now, we get to help someone just like you.
I love you, girl.

Table of Contents

Table of Contents

Acknowledgments

First and foremost, I thank the Lord for giving me a life way bigger than anything I could have done on my own, keeping Grandma Boyce as an angel to send me back, and saving me from myself. I cannot wait to keep doing your work through my existence.

To my editor Catherine Tyink. When I was ready to give up on this project, God put you in my life to save it and make it more than I ever could have imagined. Thank you for dealing with me, setting deadlines, and your essential role in bringing my story to these pages.

Thanks also to our proofreaders, Emily Arenz, Jamie Decotis, Josh Schueller, Josh Stively, Brianna Paauwe, and Leslie Autin. Your keen eyes brought this project to the next level. Thanks also to Austin Whaley at Catawba Creative for his design work and visual assistance. Thanks to Josh Lloyd for his technical support. Lastly, thanks to McFarland, my North Carolina–based publisher, for their expert guidance and support.

To my parents. Dad, for setting the standard by his example of how I should be treated, always going above and beyond for his girls. Mom, whose drive to give her girls a better life than she had while keeping us independent is what helped me become powerful. You two gave us the coolest childhood. I love you both to the moon and back.

To my friends named in this book and beyond. Thank you for playing a massive role in my life. I've been blessed with so many incredible friends. We would need to print a second book if I named them all.

My sisters, Hope and Jodi, for always believing in and encouraging me. Jodi, thank you for not beating me up too badly when we were kids. I love you both so much.

Acknowledgments

I thank everyone who supports my platform mission in real life and online. You are a massive driving force to my consistency, empathy, and motivation to keep sharing. I'm not sure I would be who I am without you.

And to you, the reader. I hope you can learn from my mistakes and apply some of these lessons to avert life's hardships. The hardships will come, but know you can persevere. If I can, you can too. Your enthusiasm means everything to me. Thank you for every message, tag, tweet, and review. And THANK YOU for reading *Power in the Roll.*

Foreword
by Amber Balcaen

One of the first times Jesi and I hung out was when we met for a coffee date to get some work done, as two driven individuals would do. Jesi picked me up, and we drove to the coffee shop. She proceeded to find a parking space.

When she pulled into a disabled parking stall, I told her, "Jesi, you can't park there; it's a handicap spot." She responded, "Amber, I can park here," and laughed out loud.

Yes, I had forgotten Jesi was in a wheelchair. There are still times that I will forget, but it's something she appreciates. When you meet Jesi, you don't see the wheelchair. You see a strong, fiery, badass woman who greets you with a huge smile and a warm hug. Someone who has turned their own identity from a victim to a victor. Something most people who have experienced adversity or trauma never achieve.

Jesi and I met through our mutual best friend, Jamie Decotis; we all love motorsports. When I found out that Jesi's mother went into labor on the day she planned to spectate a NASCAR race, it became clear why God/The Universe had brought us together. I've known Jesi for over six years. I have never seen someone experience so much personal growth in such a short time. She works this hard for herself and the betterment of others, extending beyond the disabled community.

As it is for Jesi, racing has always been a huge part of my life and escape from reality. I have raced cars for 22 years and am currently competing full-time in NASCAR's ARCA Menards series as the first Canadian female to win a sanctioned race at NASCAR. Like Jesi, I come from humble beginnings and have had to overcome much adversity to get where I am today. Our friendship was built on the foundation of similar mindsets. Our friendship continues to prove to us the importance of having like-minded individuals around you who support and uplift you while in pursuit of your greatness. Jesi's support for my dreams and how she supports everyone around her is unmatched. Jesi's discipline and consistency to be better every day are unmatched. Jesi's ability to overcome adversity and turn pain into power is, again, unmatched.

Jesi is one tough chick. She is resilient, smart, and kind but also intense, stubborn, and abrasive. She is open and vulnerable but will tell you exactly what she thinks, whether you agree with her or not. She embodies more mental toughness than anyone I know. The thing that impresses me most about Jesi is her work ethic. She accomplishes more in one day than most able-bodied people do in an entire week. Jesi strives to be the best in everything she does. She gives 110 percent in every area of her life. She is passionate and driven and has enough mental fortitude to make her success in life inevitable.

Not only is she an amazing person, but she's also an amazing friend. The kind of friend with whom you can be brutally honest and expect brutal honesty back. Not because either of us is ruthless in our approaches to friendship but because she deeply cares for others and wants the people around her to also be their best.

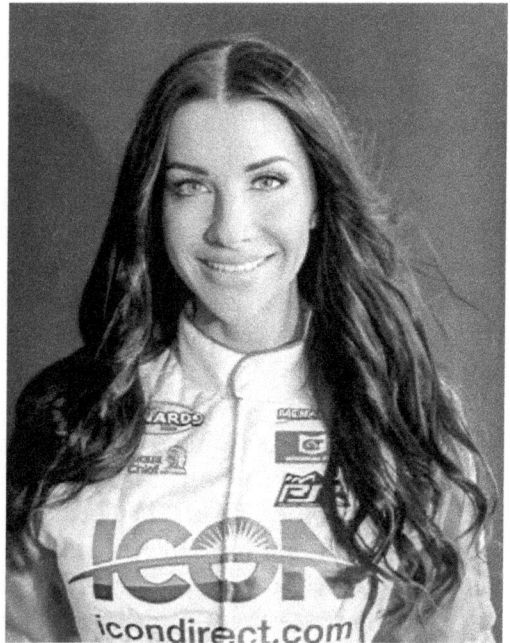

With a powerful personal story, sharp business acumen, and contagious energy, Amber Balcaen inspires audiences to push past fear, embrace challenges, and pursue their "impossible" dreams confidently and purposefully.

If you can take even half of the lessons in this book and apply them to your life, you will experience more blessings than you could ever imagine. Jesi proves that life is not about what happens to you but rather about finding the magic of perspective in your situation to improve yourself while positively impacting others.

You don't need all the tools in the toolbox to build the life of your dreams. You just need to be resourceful enough to cultivate your mental toughness by turning your positive thoughts into action while never—ever—giving up. If you can learn the skills of grit, fortitude, perseverance, self-belief, discipline, determination, and gratitude, you will live the life you've always dreamed of. Jesi has put in the work to encapsulate all of these traits. She lives by them. And she wants you to live by them too.

Amber Balcaen is a professional race car driver, entrepreneur, and motivational speaker who made history as the first Canadian female to win a NASCAR-sanctioned race in the United States. Raised in Winnipeg, Manitoba, Amber turned her dream into reality through relentless determination, grit, and resilience, securing millions in sponsorship funding and building a successful career in one of the most male-dominated sports in the world. In addition to her racing accomplishments, Amber co-founded Ask Amber, an AI tool designed to help people build mental toughness, overcome adversity, and perform at a high level. She is also the soon-to-be host of Driven, *a podcast dedicated to underdog success stories and the mindset behind achieving big goals.*

Preface

I don't know everything.
I'm not the smartest or oldest in the room.
But I've been through some things.
These things taught me a lesson in the moment
or later on after some reflection.

I hope you enjoy this literary journey as I learn
from my mistakes, consequences, and actions.
This book is not for everyone.
I cuss a little (or a lot).
I share finding my faith and how God has worked in my life.
I show you how beautiful life can be on the other side of tragedy.

This book is for those who want to do more, be more,
and live MORE.
I hope to provide you with a shortcut to unlocking your greatness.
YOU deserve to live up to your FULLEST potential.

Writing this book was not easy.
I had to take a long, hard look in the mirror.
Dig deeper than I previously thought possible.
I'm not proud of who I was or my choices,
but I've accepted myself and learned.
I no longer fear the judgment of others.
I am free.
I hope to help you find the same freedom.
Disabled or not.

Author's Note

To write this book, I relied primarily on my memories supplemented with old journals and other writings. I also asked pertinent family members and others with shared histories to provide insights and confirm my childhood memories. I've told the truth as closely as possible while acknowledging memory's cloudy filter of who I once was and who I am now. I did change the names and details of some people and events in the book to preserve their anonymity. I break away from the narrative at times to add reflective content. Reflections on my biggest life lessons. I am a coach, after all. I aim to show you the shortcut that beats going the long way every time.

PART ONE

PRE-ACCIDENT

1

Wheels

Wheels have been a theme throughout my life. I adored anything with wheels, preferably motorized for speed. Sometimes I debate myself, pondering if I was born to ride or was groomed that way from the cradle. Ultimately, the only reasonable conclusion is both nurture and nature. A natural risk-taker growing up in the perfect environment to foster it.

To paint the landscape of that environment, let's go back to my first Christmas. I was six months old and just mastering sitting up. Large hands reached into my playpen. I knew it was Dad. I could tell by the way he lifted me. Giving a gentle squeeze, he was smiling, and I smiled back. A happy, bouncy baby in her red Christmas playsuit.

In a gentle but excited voice he said, "Jesi Girl, I have a surprise for you."

We traveled to the living room, where my eyes zoomed in on something bright red. It was a pedal car, but not a generic one. This was a National Association for Stock Car Auto Racing (NASCAR) themed toy. Number 11, just like Hall of Famer Bill Elliott's former stock racing car. Dad, not bothered that I was way too young to use pedals, lowered me into the driver's seat. No need to show me what to do next. I grabbed the steering wheel with tiny hands and bit down to ease pink gums sore from teething. My first set of wheels.

You may think the story of my wheeled life began with that siren-red pedal car, but I say it started before I was born. The day my mother-to-be, Jacki, met my father-to-be, John. It started out as a normal working day. Mom sat up proud and tall, driving her long-haul 18-wheel semitruck along the highway to a new destination: Mehoopany, Pennsylvania. Mehoopany, population 1,000, is just north of the more well-known medium-sized city of Scranton.

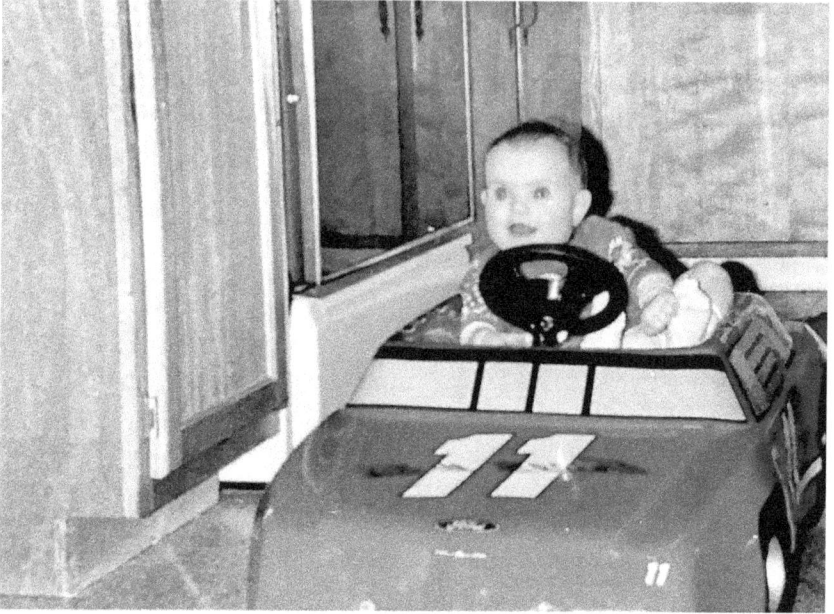

Behind the wheel of my first pedal car at six months old.

Jodi as copilot and me as the driver in our red Power Wheels Jeep.

1. Wheels

Female semitruck drivers are still uncommon today, but 35 years ago Mom was a true unicorn.

Pulling her 48-foot enclosed trailer rig into the Mehoopany-based distribution center (which happened to be my father John's company), Jacki was an unusual sight, and John noticed. The combination of her command of that semi; fiery blue eyes; and long, dark hair set his heart ablaze. Jacki, unaware of her admirer, paid no attention. She had her mind set on the day's task: load her empty trailer, collect the paperwork, and drive the highway monster to the next stop in New York. A seasoned semitruck driver, she wasted no time moving those Procter & Gamble dry products to various places around the United States. Places far away from her home in Ohio.

Parking the semi next to the dock, she walked at a fast clip to the drivers' mailboxes outside the distribution center on a mission to collect paperwork. Shoving her arm into the designated mailbox, she searched. Empty. This annoyed her as she was on a tight timeline to get back on the road. Truck drivers have a limited number of working hours when they are allowed to drive actively. Once those hours are up, they have to shut down to rest and reset.

Taking matters into her own hands, this little lady marched into the office demanding, "Where's my paperwork?! I need it now as I must get on the road!" The man at the window got flustered. "Uh, ah, I don't know what to tell you." Hearing the commotion, Dad came out of his office. Using a soothing voice, he talked her off the ledge, as he still does today. "We are so sorry, but I promise you, your paperwork will be here before they finish loading your trailer."

While John was making small talk, the friendliest sort of talk, the semi-loader arrived with Jacki's paperwork, and she was on her way. Dad was smitten. Using pull with her employer, he arranged for Mom to be frequently on the schedule dropping and hooking up in Mehoopany. A few weeks later, she was forced to stay over in Mehoopany for the night while waiting for her next trailer load.

Of course, Dad capitalized on the moment. "Jacki, would you like to have a drink after work?" All she had was her semi, so he picked her up from the hotel, and they went on their first date.

On that first date and the ones that followed, they shared the details of their lives. Good times and bad. They talked about their failed marriages. Their love of NASCAR racing, country living, and the open road. A few more dates later, Jacki started to feel butterflies in her stomach. The same giddy love John had felt at first sight. *Wow, he is so fun and easy to talk to, and we have so much in common.* A year later, my parents married in a simple ceremony. Keeping true to the roots of their romance and livelihoods, the post-ceremony get-away vehicle was a semitruck, its polished silver chrome glistening in the sunlight and hope of new beginnings.

The Mehoopany business eventually failed, so my parents packed up and moved to my mom's hometown, Canton, Ohio, for better work opportunities and to be close to my mother's family. Canton is best known for its iconic Pro Football Hall of Fame. The larger city of Akron, Ohio, is just 20 minutes north of Canton.

The Canton/Akron area is located in the center or, as Ohioans like to say, the heart of the United States. Akron, with its long history of tire manufacturing, is known as "The Rubber Capital of the World." Yes, I grew up in the land of tires. Yet another way wheels have taken center stage in my life. Settling in Canton, my

My parents on their wedding day by their semitruck.

Jodi, Mom, and me (left to right) posing in the early years.

wheel-loving parents couldn't stay away from trucking. Dad went on to be a dispatcher in Akron, Ohio. My mom was looking for another long-haul semitruck driving job when she found out she was pregnant with me, so she pulled the brakes on that.

The day I was born, my parents had plans to leave for a NASCAR race in Michigan. That morning, my mom calmly said, "John, it's time." Dad thought Mom's comment meant it was time to leave for the NASCAR race, but she clarified, "It's time to leave for the hospital. This baby is ready."

Dad couldn't believe it. I was born on Father's Day, the exact day the doctor predicted. What a way to celebrate. They decided to name me Jesi Michele Stracham. Not Jessica or Jesse but simply Jesi, a name suitable for a boy or girl. Michele with only one "l" because, as Mom explained, she wasn't big on wasting letters. After me, they became parents again in short order, my sister Jodi entering the world 13 months after me. Mom barely caught her breath after each birth, returning to her semi and long-distance driving weeks after each of us was born.

Part One—Pre-Accident

To avoid daycare, my parents started their own trucking business in the basement of our house. That way, Dad could work, control Mom's schedule, and keep one eye on Jodi and me. This left us off doing our own thing most of the time. It is always the two of us together. I have no memories of growing up without Jodi by my side. My second sister, Hope, was Mom's biological daughter from a teen pregnancy. Mom's older sister raised Hope. Hope joined the basement business as an employee after she turned 25. She would become like a second mother when our mom was driving, making sure we didn't tear the house down.

My earliest memory is watching Mom through the window as she drove her semitruck into our expansive parking lot or, as she called it, a one-way horseshoe of a driveway. A horseshoe because the long driveway in front of our corner house was U-shaped with two main road entrances on each end. A long, large driveway in theory but only as wide as the semitruck. Jodi and I peered out the window or sat in the yard, observing Mom snake her semitruck, carefully

Hope (right) and me in the car.

pulling her long trailer in and out of the horseshoe between multiday trips. I missed my mom. I missed her affection and attention. A feeling of longing is my second earliest memory.

Not having a mom for long periods was something I accepted, the way kids do. Still, her absence and Dad's preoccupation with work left me without supervision—no rules—so I took full advantage and then some. My baby walk quickly became a run. I tore through our house in tornado fashion, moving fast from one room to the next, leaving a signature trademark of mess and chaos. This earned me several childhood nicknames from my parents and Hope: Messy Jesi, Dirt Magnet, and Spoiled Brat. Dad, seeing my aggressive nature, did not ridicule me for it. Instead, he gave me outlets for all that energy. Whatever my fickle heart wanted, it got. I believed I deserved it, too. After all, I was a Spoiled Brat.

Spoiling was highlighted early. When I tossed aside the NASCAR pedal car, Dad came through again, hooking me up with a battery-powered toy Jeep. An expensive luxury item for a family of modest income. Jodi and I beamed at the happy surprise. It was designed for bigger, older kids, and my petite body couldn't reach the pedals. Not big on age requirements for anything, Dad got straight to work rigging a thick wooden block on top of the gas pedal for my convenience. Next, to contain us, he added a hose clamp to the steering wheel, forcing the Jeep to move only in circles.

There I was, still in diapers but riding on four wheels. Hands on the steering wheel and foot on the gas, I made circle after circle until I fell asleep, the battery died, or both. Toddler Jeep was much more than a symbol of my tomboyish nature and indulgent parents. Looking closely at me as the little one with wispy brown hair and a big, baby-toothed grin spinning round and round like a wheel myself, you would get a good dose of foreboding of some of what was to come.

Trouble grew in proportion to each of my birthdays. Not long after Jodi came home from the hospital, I pulled her car seat off the counter with her in it. I made the poor baby cry. I threw my Barbie dolls around. Dad came home from the toy store with the nicest Barbie dolls—the full-size, brand-name ones with matching clothing and bendable parts.

He would hand me a new Barbie, and the lovely new doll would go from his safe hands to my unsafe hands with one parental request. "Jesi, please take good care of your new doll."

Shaking my head yes, I'd grab the doll from Dad's hands. Next, I'd run off, searching for scissors and permanent markers. *Chop, Chop!* Barbie's hair would get cut off before I added makeup with marker. Eventually, after a few repeat offenses and not wanting to waste money, Dad started picking up the cheaper versions from the Dollar Store. The kind of cheap where the heads pop right off when you play with them. That didn't matter; they were getting destroyed like the others. Once satisfied with Barbie's look, I would take the same scissors to my hair, hacking it off regularly. So often Mom and Dad eventually gave up and let me do it.

Anything I could do to alter my appearance, I tried. I started cutting my hair as soon as I mastered using adult scissors, which was before kindergarten. Once I started school, I added to the look with makeup and a creative dressing style. Tomboyish, yet I mixed and matched however I pleased.

Bored with hacking at my hair, I decided to bleach it blonde. Back then, there was no YouTube tutorial or Googling to figure out home bleaching. I assumed household bleach would do the trick. *It's all the same, right?* My friend Macy, my sister, and I grabbed one of my mom's big cooking bowls and the white jug of household bleach and quickly hurried upstairs to start the process. I held my breath before plunging my head into the clear bleach. The smell was awful while my scalp tingled and the bleach gradually turned my hair a weird orangish tone. Hands on head, I could tell the texture was different too: dry, fried, and sticky.

When I got sick of walking around with sticky, orange hair, I asked Mom, "Can I get started on real hair dye?" She agreed. "All right. Let's go to the store and get boxed hair dye in your natural color."

This started a routine of altering my hair, and I tried all kinds of crazy cuts and colors—grass and dirt stains on my clothes from practically living outdoors adding to the effect. I never looked like the sweet little girl next door. I was the one who got side glances from other moms as they held onto their children just a little tighter.

My parents, dealing with my rebellious nature, couldn't give Jodi as much attention. We were sisters who shared common interests while approaching life from different points of view. Deep inside, I wanted to be more like Jodi. To be good. Instead, it was always an internal struggle to make the right decision. Often, I would picture that invisible good Jodi-like angel on one of my shoulders, whispering in my ear to listen to my parents and follow the rules. On the other shoulder was that less-defined bad angel who told me to break all the rules. More often than not, the dark angel side was the direction I took without regard to the consequences. To me, it was all about the fun. Fun meant taking chances, exploring boundaries, and being independent.

2

Big Wheels

In Ohio, there were two places I could be free. One was the small Canton South neighborhood where we spent most days, and the other was the campground. A campground called Harrison Hills. Harrison Hills was in Carrollton, about an hour away from our house. My parents bought a lot in Harrison Hills on a neighbor's recommendation. Dropping a camper on our lot with a simple roof over the structure, we spent campground weekends riding everything. Golf carts, go-karts, and motorized dirt bikes from April to September. It was at the campground where I could be my full tomboy self. Dad, who loved wheeled toys like I did, kept the supply coming.

When I was seven, we found out I am deathly allergic to poison oak, sumac, and ivy. It was the weekend, and I was building a fort in the woods at camp. Suddenly my entire body broke out in hives and swelled up. Even my throat constricted, making it harder to breathe. They put me on steroids to help clear it up. Those steroids did something to my little child's brain. On steroids, my bratty personality really came out. I acted like a maniac.

Going back to camp straight from the doctor's office, swollen face and all, I took my helmet and launched it across our campsite, screaming at my mom, "This helmet isn't fucking good enough!"

Yes, as a small child, I was dropping F-bombs. My parents shook their heads in dismay at their foul-mouthed daughter while a faint smile formed on my devil lips. I took pleasure in their pain. I stay away from those plants to this day. Some things in childhood are impossible to forget. We rotated our fun between the neighborhood and the campground, where our family's collection of high-powered toys kept growing.

Adding to my personal stash, Dad built me a mini Grand Prix

2. Big Wheels

My custom Jeff Gordon Dupont Go-Kart.

My 350cc Yamaha Warrior.

Dupont go-kart. A one-of-a-kind go-kart with a complex, custom paint job Dad did himself using a spray gun and some tape. The ultimate Dad gift. A little replica version of NASCAR driver Jeff Gordon's rainbow-painted Dupont car. The famous number 24 Jeff Gordon because Dad knew he was my favorite driver. On day one of my new gift, I rode that little go-kart as fast as possible, driving it into our swing set, bending its frame so much it was never the same. On another day, I crashed it into Jodi's go-kart. This sent both her and her cart rolling down the dirt path. Ultimately, within the first year, I trashed my mini Grand Prix. Man, how I loved that go-kart. Until I didn't. Then it was on to the next thing—a girl in perpetual motion.

Bored with our motorized toys, Jodi and I, now in second and third grade, respectively, begged and pleaded to convince Dad to get us all-terrain vehicles—also known as ATVs, four-wheelers, or quads—using the classic kid argument: "Come on, everyone else at camp has them. Why can't we? Please!" We kept asking until he relented, as he always did for his girls.

Our first ATVs were small Polaris Scrambler 90cc or mini quads. Not wanting to leave Mom out, Dad bought her a full-size, full-power Polaris Sportsman 350. One rainy morning, after waking up, our whole family headed out to a restaurant for breakfast. My parents had forgotten something, so we turned around and went back home. Away for just a few minutes, we noticed that the trailer holding our toys was wide open. The lawnmower and mini quads lay outside in odd places. Inspecting the trailer, we knew Mom's Polaris ATV was stolen. Tracking down that four-wheeler was a wild chase for months. No luck. To replace it, Dad bought Mom a Suzuki z400. A very fast quad with a lot of torque. She picked the Suzuki not for speed but because, she said, it looked like a praying mantis. Mom had no idea how much power the quad had, but I did. When Mom was away, Dad made the mistake of letting us ride Mom's new quad a few times, which was a blast because of how easily it popped into a wheelie compared to our smaller mini quad ATVs.

After tasting mom's Suzuki z400, I got my own upgrade on my ninth birthday. Ditching the 90cc mini quad for a full adult-sized Yamaha 350 Warrior. It was an extravagant birthday gift, especially for a fourth grader. I ran off to use it without a glance back to say thank you. The Warrior was a tank compared to the z400. It was heavy and slower than Mom's Suzuki, making it harder to pop wheelies and maneuver. It was better than that mini quad, though. I rode it until the wheels fell off.

When not on the Warrior, I joined the other kids to terrorize the campground for most of the summer playing golf cart tag. Dividing up guys against girls, boys piled on one cart, and the girls jammed into the other cart. Most golf carts have a governor to slow them down, controlling them for safety. Our dads, all novice mechanics, removed ours. We were wide open to chase one another around at high speeds, taking them down hills, popping wheelies, and playing tag.

After a round of golf cart tag, it was time to hit up Shale Pit. Shale Pit contained natural jumps highlighted by a massive dip deep enough to collect about 12 inches of water inside shale rock bowls. We made a game of going as fast as we could on our gas-powered four-wheelers, driving down the massive gravel roadway that led up and through the pit. Our goal was to hydroplane over the massive water dip, tires hitting the ground hard before cruising the downhill portion of the roadway.

We often doubled up on our ATV quads, riding two at a time. Lauren, a friend from the campground, was my partner in crime. We doubled up, driving recklessly. As a pair, we rode our ATVs through three or four passes before flying over Shale Pit. Once, after a few laps, we decided to go one more time. "One more time" was something I often said while doing crazy driving stunts. I couldn't get enough of the adrenaline rush.

On this last pass, we hydroplaned over the puddle, cresting the hill just as another friend turned around on the other side. We smashed into him. I flew off the quad while Lauren flew into the ditch, my Yamaha Warrior four-wheeler flying close behind. It happened fast. Before we knew it, the friend we hit had to get his groin stitched up. We totaled the Warrior, completely bending the frame. No worries though, since Lauren's dad and my dad worked together late into the night over a case of beer, swapping out the bent frame to put the quad back together. Soon it was good as new, ready for me to destroy again.

Rollercoaster Hill, as we called it, was another campground highlight. A steep grade of rolling hills formed a series of three hills that went up and down like a roller coaster. Getting as much speed as possible on our bicycles, we attacked those hills. The hilly roads were a mixture of gravel and pavement. I came in full speed ahead, catching air before dropping into the hill. I hit a patch of gravel, and the bicycle's back tire washed out. I wasn't wearing a helmet, and the back of my head hit the ground. I was rushed to urgent care. The gash was massive. Picking through, urgent care staff got most of the gravel out of the wound before sending me on my way. There's still a lump in the back of my head to remind me of the time I blew off the simple step of putting on a helmet.

Bored with Shale Pit and Rollercoaster Hill, a fellow camper at Harrison Hills built a small sand packed drag racing track, about 30 feet long, located beside the lodge housing the campground pool. I alternated between racing our golf cart and my full-size four-wheeler on that track over and over, and racing quickly rose to the top of my favorite camp activities. I thrived on the competition, and, to my delight, Jodi loved it as much as I did. We raced each other; we raced other kid campers; we even raced adults.

Riding and racing at camp, we heard about other drag races outside our little weekend community—real races with cash prizes and a much longer 300-foot hard-packed dirt drag strip. Even though I was only 11 and Jodi was 10, we wanted in. After all, we had been racing informally at the campground for about a year. Long enough to figure out we were pretty good at it. Using the usual tactic, we started begging Dad. "Dad, please, Jodi and I are ready. Sign us up!"

Unable to say no to his girls, Dad entered us into our first official competition. To prepare, Dad had our full-sized four-wheelers lowered and modified to run on a fuel source called alcohol. The final touch came next. He installed a protective wheelie bar on the back of each to stop them from flipping over.

The morning before my first race, I could barely wait to leave camp and head to the track. In the early afternoon, we loaded our ATVs into our red hauling trailer hooked to Dad's big truck. He drove us about an hour away from camp into the backwoods of the Ohio–West Virginia border. I didn't know what to expect exactly as I had never seen or been to a real drag race. Unless you count watching *Top Fuel*, a drag racing television show.

The entry fee was $15 for each category. Dad signed us up for three categories each, starting with the "open" class. Cash prizes depended on how many people were in a class. Arriving at that first race, my eyes went to the twinkling Christmas tree–style lights centered between two lanes of dirt track. Scanning our competition, I noticed something else. Jodi and I were two of only three girls racing. That part I expected; there aren't many females in the sport. The big surprise was we were the only kids. I was in sixth grade, and Jodi was in fifth. All the other competitors were adults. Grown-ups ranging between 20 and 60.

Our hearts pounded as we lined our ATVs up on the starting line, head to hip with a field of men. Adrenaline was pumping, but we weren't scared. Not us. We enjoyed being the underdogs. Sisters with new souped-up toys itching to unleash their power. I was revved and ready when the stage lights illuminated the Christmas tree. Heart racing, I moved to the starting line with one opponent. We were to race in randomly assigned pairs, competing with the whole field against the clock. I kept a laser focus on the lights. Eight pre-stage white lights lit up, four on each side, indicating that my opponents and I were ready to race—the next three yellow lights followed by two green ones.

My strategy was simple. Don't jump the line before the green lights go, or you will be red-lighted, an automatic loss of that pass. Going hard, I quickly jammed through the gears to accelerate to top speed. I stayed laser focused, eyes locked on the finish line. Jodi and I did well, each winning a small prize towards the front of the pack. Afterward, on the way home, we agreed that drag racing was our form of quality family time. What a blast. I loved wheeled competition. *This is way better than school sports*, I thought to myself.

The races were by process of elimination. You would move through the bracket until two were left to win the cash prize. Jodi was always better than I was on the lights, so when we raced each other early on, she would quickly take me out of the race. Gaining experience, we eventually rose to the top of the ranks, commonly securing first or second places. Jodi and I credit much of our drag racing success to our being sober. The adults were drinking beer, whiskey, or other forms of alcohol throughout each event. Men didn't enjoy getting beat by two little girls, but we enjoyed delivering the beating.

Part One—Pre-Accident

One day, the race promoter told my dad, "John, the guys don't like getting beat by your girls. Most of the men are threatening to boycott the track if they don't quit coming. I'm sure they can find something else to do." In response, Dad shrugged his shoulders. "Okay, I will find somewhere else for us to race." The following weekend, we were on a new drag strip. Strachams are a lot of things, but we aren't quitters.

3

My Time

"The desire of the lazy man kills him, for his hands refuse to labor."
—Proverbs 21:25 New King James Version

Beads of sweat dripped down my forehead in the warm Ohio summer sunshine as I sat on my parents' riding lawn mower. A small yet mighty figure at 13 years old, I felt the way many teenagers do. Pissed off a good deal of the time. Especially when it came to doing anything considered a chore, such as mowing the lawn. The upside was that it was a riding lawn mower, so I rode with gusto, full throttle, and in circles around the house, pretending I was in a race. After a few spins on my self-made racetrack, you could see the circular dirt path forming around the house. Being particular about the appearance of her yard, Mom was not happy. She peered out the sunroom windows, frustrated.

Resembling a racing spectator, she yelled something different each time I made a lap and got within earshot. "Jesi, slow down; you're going too fast!" "Jesi, you're missing a lot of the lawn!" "You're not doing it right!"

I heard the words, but my adolescent brain ignored them and I kept going. I liked my little game, spinning in circles, even if no one else was playing. After I repeated the same offense a few more times, Mom grew tired of the ugly yard and fruitless fight. Rather than try to control me, she hired professionals who left nice lines rather than a dirt circle track.

Dad was a regular smoker and had a habit of smoking throughout the day, indoors and outside. Watching him, I learned the basics of smoking and decided to try it. I started by using a piece of hay straw as a cigarette. Bored with play smoking on the hay straw, I snuck into the office basement one night, where Dad worked and smoked, looking for the real thing. My eyes zoomed in on the glass ashtrays in the workstation. Quickly and quietly, I grabbed the discarded cigarette butts from the ashtrays, dropping them into my pants pocket for safekeeping. Later, I'd smoke those stolen butts under pine trees in our backyard, away from prying eyes. The more I smoked, the more I enjoyed it. This routine went on unnoticed for a whole year, until I was 14 and happened to be upstairs in the house when everyone else was outside.

Emboldened from practicing my smoking skills on the short discards, I found Dad's cigarette stash and gently pulled one out of an open pack. Considering options, I rejected the safer one of going somewhere outside to smoke. *It seems like too much effort.* Instead, I walked upstairs to my bathroom, turned on the shower, and lit up. I knew that anyone who walked into that bathroom after me might smell it. Yet, in my child's mind, I rationalized the shower as the safest location. *For sure the steam from the hot shower will take away the smoke. Plus, the right time was my time. The right place was whatever I wanted it to be.* Smoking that first full cigarette started my on-and-off smoking habit. Smoking stuck with me. Once I hit 18, I smoked consistently up until the day I became paralyzed four years later.

Cigarettes weren't the only thing I lit up. As a growing preteen, I was hungry a lot. Once, I wanted a baked potato, and I wanted it immediately. I knew nothing about cooking potatoes, but I didn't want to wait for the oven to warm up. *That would take at least an hour.* Instead, I put it in the microwave without cutting it up or poking holes in it. Guessing, I punched high power for 10 minutes before going upstairs. After a few minutes, Dad noticed sparks of flame shooting off my potato. I nearly set the kitchen on fire. Catching it just in time, Dad fumed.

I heard him yelling up the steps, "Who the fuck put a whole potato in the microwave?! How long was it cooking?! You almost burnt the house down!"

Unaffected, I glanced at him from the top of the stairs, rolled my eyes, and shrugged my shoulders. "Jeez, Dad, I just wanted to eat a baked potato."

I've burned my world down a few times by not practicing patience. The potato was me just getting started.

Another place where I defied the rules was Nimishillen Creek, a large miles-long creek near our house. It's a tributary of the Sandy Creek that stretches through Ohio, part of the Mississippi River watershed. To look at Nimishillen Creek in the summertime, you would think it was a heavenly swimming or tubing spot. While I saw no issues with it, my parents knew that less than a mile up the creek was the city's water treatment plant. At the time, questionable plant water ran into the Nimishillen, so my parents asked us not to swim in it.

One of the neighborhood dads hung a long, thick rope swing for us to swing into that river during the warm summer days. In spite of my parents' rule and warning, I was all in. The routine was a simple one: First I'd tell Dad I was going somewhere else, then we'd ride our bikes down to the rope swing and play with the neighborhood kids in the contaminated water for hours. I never got caught. *What they don't know won't hurt them*, I thought to myself with satisfaction.

Regarding childhood best friends, I had my sister, Lauren from the campground, and Macy from my Canton neighborhood. Macy shared my passion for outdoor mischief, while Lauren and Jodi were more levelheaded rule followers. Macy and I referred to them as "Goody Two-Shoes." I don't remember what they called us on the off chance the four of us weren't together, but because of our differences, Jodi and Lauren spent a bit more time together, leaving Macy and me on our own. Macy's house was just a few miles down the road from us. Macy and I had sleepovers often, mostly at my house or the campground. When Macy's parents divorced, we were nearly inseparable.

One day, a boy at school stole a bicycle and ditched it at our house. We spray-painted it black, making the "hot" bicycle unrecognizable. Macy said, "Hey Jesi, look. It has pegs to stand on mounted in the back!" Excited to ride it, I didn't hesitate. "Cool. Let's go!"

I rode all over Canton, Macy perched on the handlebars or the back pegs. We were going fast, and Macy fell off the back of the bike, scraping up her leg enough for it to bleed. Not bothered, she jumped right back on, and we continued our mission to explore. Between biking and sneaking out, I knew she was the friend for me—my partner in crime.

A special adventure-worthy space for us was a massive structure down the road from our house in an area known as the Old North industry. Before it became defunct and fell apart board by board, it was a church that included remnants of a school that Mom had attended years before. There were desks and even ratty stuffed animals in a broken claw machine. Musky, dusty, and unsafe, it was a three-story structure with boarded-up windows and plenty of room to explore if you were gutsy enough to enter.

Macy, Lauren, Jodi, and I approached the old building, largely intact yet super creepy because of the pitch-black darkness inside; the electricity had gone permanently out years earlier. We checked the door. Locked tight. Of course, that didn't stop us. We got in through broken windows and slid our small frames through boarded-up doors finagled open.

The city of Canton hadn't done a great job ensuring that the place was buttoned up. We could see that homeless people had been squatting on the floors above the former worship area. That day it was empty. We messed around in the pews and played hide-and-seek in the rafters. It was pretty harmless stuff, but, looking back, it was also quite gutsy for middle school kids. Suddenly, our reign inside was disturbed. Adults came into the main worship area while we scrambled to hide among the pews. The intruders started yelling as they paraded down the hallway, slamming the locker doors. "You kids need to get out of here. This place is ours!" Terrified, we quivered until they finally left.

I'm sure our tormentors found the situation hilarious. I led our little kid gang back several more times, and we had the best time facing our fears and exploring the old building.

Around the same time, Macy, Jodi, and I were deep into a pre-teen phase calling ourselves "Three Girls and a Video Camera." During school breaks, Lauren stayed with us, and we all became young content creators before content creation was a thing. Armed with a video camera my parents had given me for Christmas, our purpose was born. We made goofy, slapstick-style humor videos and transferred the recordings to a VHS tape for viewing. For readers too young to know, the letters in VHS stand for Video Home System. Invented in the 1970s, VHS was the widely used nickname for the small analog black cassette tapes made of hard plastic you'd place in the video camera. After recording, you would transfer the black VHS tape into a VHS player and then play your movie.

3. My Time

Three Girls and a Video Camera's first stunt was riding our skateboards down the hill by the bus garage. Instead of standing on the board, we sat on it, riding down on our butts, hitting the sewage grate in the middle of the hill to catch some air before landing or wiping it out on the other side. Beside the bus garage, they stored those massive plastic drainpipes you could walk through. Armed with our skateboards and my camera, we alternated between skating through the tubes and using a board to go over the tubes from one end to the other.

In the summer, camera ready, we moved the trampoline as close to the garage as possible. Yes, we had a trampoline. A big one, with no safety nets. We would all pile on, counting down "3, 2, 1, go!" and jumping together so it would launch one of us high enough to grab the garage roof and pull up into a standing position. Once upright, we'd jump off the roof onto the trampoline, sending the other girls flying. After several jumps and catching air, we lay on the trampoline laughing.

In the winter, we filmed sledding on a steep, snowy hill with a small stream at the very bottom. Steep enough that my parents would disapprove if they had been there to see it. I led the charge, focusing on hitting a tree stump sticking out of the snow. The stump had the shape of a wooden ramp, like a ski jump. I wanted everything to do with hitting that ramp, so I went for it. The girls cheered hard, hyping me up while I sledded the hill at full speed. Hitting the stump, I flew several feet before dropping into the streambed, just like you'd see in an old *Road Runner* cartoon.

One time, I hit the creek bed hard and screamed into the camera, "Ahh, I broke my back!" As it turned out, I did not break my back. That would come later, 10 years later. Sometimes I wonder if my future manifested all those years ago, when I declared my back as broken. I sure wish we still had that tape of my epic crash.

When we weren't racing or screwing around with the camera, there was school. Living close by, Macy and I had been together since kindergarten. Whenever Macy slept over on school nights, the chances were high that Macy, Jodi, and I would stay up late talking, sleep in, and miss the school bus. Watching the school bus rolling away without us, Dad would get mad. Fortunately, Faircrest Middle School wasn't too far, just over a mile from our house following the back roads. Gathering our things for the day, the three of us would hoof it. Our shortcut, which involved parking lots and cut through the woods, popped us out in the back of the middle school.

4

Fast Lane

Middle school rolled into high school. Canton South High School. Our house was even closer to the high school, so every morning I walked myself to school, passing through the bus garage parking lot, tennis courts, and football field. Sometimes a friend would join me. I always walked to high school with some swagger, an air of coolness. I was known by then as "the girl who raced four-wheelers."

In middle school, Jodi and I stopped informal drag racing and started Grand National Cross Country (GNCC) series racing. By high school I was totally into GNCC. The competition is similar to motocross, but instead of using an enclosed racetrack, you race in extended off-road courses eight to 12 miles long through wooded plots of land. GNCC races are known for being physically demanding, lasting up to three hours. They are also huge events. Up to 2,200 riders speed through tracks in the woods, hills, mud, rocks, roots, motocross track sections, and more.

Where Jodi was better on the short-course drag races of our younger years, the woods were my thing. I tore through the woods fearless and determined to win. Never hurting myself or breaking a bone added to my cocky attitude. Walking to high school, I'd be thinking about racing. Everything in my mind was tied back to racing. Off-road racing was my whole identity. If I couldn't ride and race, nothing else in life would matter. I wouldn't exist. We often turn the things we love and are most passionate about into our sole identity. We are more than our hobbies, struggles, and abilities; as a kid, I didn't see myself as anything or anyone beyond a racer. Racing and being boy crazy was where I landed, and I sunk in deep.

While I kept my laser focus on racing, it turned out I wouldn't be the only Stracham studying high school content. Just before I entered ninth grade, Mom made a decision. "Since Jesi is starting high school, I might as well get my diploma too."

Motivated to escape a dysfunctional home situation, Mom had dropped out of high school before even starting, at age 13. My feisty, independent mother saved a bit of babysitting money, packed her backpack, and walked to the highway. There she put her thumb out, hitchhiking across the country alone from Canton, Ohio, to San Francisco, California. Mom's decision to finish school was a surprise but not entirely unexpected.

Growing up, we heard Mom tell us, other family members, and friends, "I have no regrets about running away, but I do regret not finishing high school."

In tandem with me, she worked through math, science, social studies, and English, cramming studies in between long-haul semi-driving. At the end of my ninth grade year, Mom took the high school equivalency exam and passed. On graduation day, our whole family beamed with pride watching my triumphant mother walk across the stage at a neighboring high school's graduation ceremony. At age 50, she finally got her diploma.

High school life consisted of school during the week and races on the weekends. More to the point, extended weekends. I missed a lot of school for racing, but I didn't care. Studies were meaningless since I wasn't a student. I was a GNCC quad racer. In ninth grade, caring more about my looks than ever, I wore a neutral graphic long-sleeve shirt on school picture day. This was the first school picture in years I didn't wear my racing jersey, which was my personal school uniform worn for important races and special events. That year I was trying to be cute, opting for something more fashionable. But, somehow, I still looked like a tomboy.

When I watched movies, it was always a movie about dirt bike racing, especially *Motocross* on the Disney Channel. Posters of some of my favorite GNCC ATVs and dirt bike riders hung all over my bedroom walls. I wanted to be like Traci Pickens. *Traci is living the dream*, I thought. She had a full, Yamaha-sponsored ride and was the baddest woman on four wheels in the GNCC series.

Between high school and racing, a sport dominated by guys, I suddenly had a heterosexual teenage girl's playground. Hormones raged as my interest in the opposite gender grew. The adrenaline rush I felt around an attractive guy rivaled the rush I felt racing. I loved males in an aggressive way, not unlike the way I approached racing. And when I say "love," I'm not talking about a romantic type of love. I wasn't looking for my prince; a long-term, loving relationship; or even someone to treat me as a friend. I loved guys like a fox loves chickens, hunting them the same. It was the instant pleasure from male attention I was after. My thoughts and fantasies focused on aesthetics and presentation. Broad chests, large muscles, aversion to too much talking, and preference for just getting on with things. Being liked was also important. If a boy looked my way, I felt better about myself. I wanted to be wanted and lusted after.

Yes, I was boy crazy. Mom has a bold, wild side. Maybe I

I was "sex, drugs, and rock & roll" before I understood what that meant.

From right to left, Macy, Jodi, and me, circa 2007–2008.

inherited that from her. Maybe my drive for attention had something to do with a lack of attention from my preoccupied parents. I don't know precisely why, but sexually I loved to please and allow boys to please me. I got aggressive in seeking male attention and craved the sensation of being sexual. I placed my energy into boys, especially when it came to getting their attention. I fed my addiction by being wherever men were, hanging out with them, smiling big, talking dirty, using sarcastic humor, and presenting with a flirty "I'm up for anything" demeanor. My fix.

The mature version of me now knows her worth. Recognizing my worth wasn't easy because I had long measured my value by how much temporary validation men—any man—gave me. Not unlike cigarettes, prescription drugs, and alcohol, which also were starting to take center stage in my life, sex was one of many self-destructive vices I dabbled in. It was my favorite vice to indulge in shamelessly.

While I hooked up with plenty of guys in some form, there was only one man I ever cared about in high school: Soldier Boy. I met him at my friend's birthday party. He was her older brother, a senior, and we were all freshmen. When I say I met Soldier Boy, I mean the moment I saw him, I was a hormone-crazed teenager, instantly wanting to be his girl. And by "be his girl," I mean "sleep with him." Yes, I considered myself sexually experienced by 14. I had over a year of experience under my belt by that time, convinced I knew how to please my male counterpart. Call it attraction or hormones, but I wanted to know this boy deeply.

Without hesitation, I asked my friend, "Is he single?" She told me, "He just broke up with his high school sweetheart." *Perfect. Time to go in for the kill.* Suddenly obsessed, I left my poor friend—at her birthday party!—to flirt with her brother for the duration. Then I spent the next three months pining away from afar when I noticed another girl in my grade hanging out with him. *I'm getting my way even if I have to force it,* I vowed, and decided to fight her between classes. *The bitch is going down.* To prepare for the fight, I took my earrings out and put my hair up, waiting for the first-period bell. When the bell rang, I ran down the stairs of the high school straight to her locker.

"You're a skank!" I opened.

Before the surprised and confused girl could finish her response—"I'm a skank...?!"—I hit her.

It wasn't much of a fight. We both got a few extra days of spring break in the form of out-of-school suspension. I truly didn't care about the suspension. *Whatever, I did what had to be done.*

The strategy worked. Soldier Boy appreciated my efforts, and by the end of ninth grade we were hanging out as a couple (or as much of a couple as any two high school kids can be). We agreed I would go to his house to hook up. Easy decision since his bedroom was in the basement, isolated from the rest of the house. Less chance of getting caught.

I considered how to execute our plan. I knew better than to sneak out when my mom was home because she had eyes in the back of her head and never missed anything. That special mom-sense that knows when things aren't right. Instead of risking it when she was home, I waited for those days she was over the road. *Sorry Dad, but you sleep deeper and are easier to fool.*

Since my bedroom was on the second story, I needed a plan to safely exit without being noticed. My parents installed an alarm system shortly after the quads were stolen, so I couldn't walk through the front door without the alarm system notifying the house. It had to appear like I was still in bed sleeping. Ohio weather is pleasant in the spring, so I knew I'd manage with a sweatshirt, light jacket, and tennis shoes—no need to worry about grabbing a coat or boots.

Discovering I could pull the top of my bedroom window down to bypass the home's alarm system, I quietly opened it up. Testing the waters, I stretched over to the adjacent roof. It took a huge leap to get there, and as I leaped, I wondered if I would sprain my ankle, break something, or worse, fall to the ground within the open space between my window and the roof. There was a gap because there was no roof directly under the window. I had to take a risky leap to get to the nearest roof, which was another part of the house.

Fear and common sense should have stopped me, but I'm not wired that way. I didn't even bother with a flashlight to better gauge the distance. Taking that chance, I made it. It was a relief to land as quietly as possible and feel the sturdy roof under my feet. Once on the sunroom roof, I knew I'd find a brick ledge halfway down the side wall, so I scaled that part, getting first to the ledge and then scaling the rest using the porch swing as needed for support to reach solid ground. I felt proud. *If there's a will*, I thought, *there's a way.*

Walking the lonely mile down the road in darkness to Soldier Boy's house, I smiled. *Not only did I make it, but the water bottle in my hand did, too.* It was a boozy bottle, filled earlier from my parents' fully stocked bar in the basement. At the bar, I had found a large bottle of a whiskey scotch blend I knew Soldier Boy would enjoy. Once my water bottle was full of booze, I had "replaced" what I stole with water so my parents wouldn't notice. Gift-giving is my love language. *Gifts will show him that I care*, I thought, *and this will keep him in my life longer.*

Expecting me, he let me in quickly, taking me down to his basement bedroom. We stayed up all night partaking in adult activities before I walked home to get ready for school in the wee hours of the morning. Reaching my yard, I snuck back into the house before Dad got up. It was an adrenaline rush and a miracle I never got caught or kidnapped on those dark, lonely walks to and from my house.

I completed this routine several nights a week until the end of ninth grade. Eventually, after I leaned on my bedroom window roughly a few times while getting out, the top part of the window broke and it would no longer close after I snuck out. This meant I had to find another window to use to bypass the alarm. I scanned the house for another exit before settling on the window in the laundry room. It was the most secluded area of the house and the safest spot to exit quietly. Plus, it had a handy stand for the dog bowls that I could use as a step stool to help boost me over the top. Fun fact: My husky Roxanne uses that same bowl today.

Sometimes I approached our house in the early dawn hours to discover Mom's semitruck in the driveway. I wasn't expecting her, but she was home. I'd always panic. She was the last person I wanted to catch me. Fortunately—or unfortunately, depending on your perspective—she never did.

Soldier Boy and I broke up in classic dramatic high school fashion. At the end of my ninth grade year, he graduated and left for military basic training several hundred miles away. We parted ways on good terms with no hard feelings. As for his sister, I'm pretty sure she hated my guts for ditching her on her birthday to run off with her brother. I can't say I wouldn't have felt the same way if a friend did something like that to me. I was a bit of a shithead back then.

Soldier Boy was gone. I felt empty inside, all alone. Shortly after he left, I missed my period and thought, *Oh my God. Play adult games and win adult prizes.* Scared, I told Lauren and Jodi. Lauren's older sister was of driving age, so she recruited her to help me. They picked me up at my house, using the excuse that we were going to go to Cedar Point, a big amusement park in Sandusky, Ohio. Instead, we went to the pharmacy, my legs shaking and hands wringing. Lauren's older sister bought a pregnancy test, and we returned to Lauren's parents' house. I took the test. After waiting for what seemed like an eternity, I saw faint lines start to form on the indicator. To my horror, positive. I was 15. Fifteen and pregnant. MTV's reality series suddenly became my reality. My heart raced inside my chest as I left Lauren's house for home.

Since Soldier Boy was incommunicado during basic training, I told his family. They weren't thrilled but also weren't angry. My family was another story. I told my family as a group. I will never forget my mom and Hope's reactions. In firm tones, they each told me that the tradition of teen pregnancies would not continue in the Stracham family. My mom was a teen parent when she had Hope. Hope then had her oldest child as a late teen. Pure passion formed Mom's words: "We will not be doing this."

Mom and I went to the doctor for a vaginal ultrasound. I had been busy giving my body away, but something about a camera inside me felt exceedingly violating. I was still young, having experienced a pap smear and vaginal exam just once before. I was new to the women's health routine, which I'm sure contributed to my discomfort. All I could do was hold on to the cold, steel side rail to stop myself from leaping off the table and running. Then, there it was on the ultrasound screen. Pregnancy. After the ultrasound, I was told it was a nonviable tubular pregnancy. For my physical safety, I would have to abort the fetus. I was not convinced this was true, but I asked no questions. For once, I did exactly what I was told.

If I could have jumped on a quad and raced my problems away, I would have. Instead, they gave me two pills orally and four vaginally. The time after was the worst. For a full month, I had to wear diapers due to the blood loss. During the most intense part, I was losing chunks of mass. It was terrifying. I never did address the mental side of that experience. It was so traumatic that I buried the experience and my feelings about it deep down. I never talked about this dark, shameful secret except in passing. Instead, I tried my best to forget. Forgetting in a way that it was never fully processed.

By tenth grade, attempting to push away my past, I was ready for something new. Experimenting, I dated a girl named Ashley for one day. We went to an event for her dad's work together. After a few hours of hanging out, she took me home. Before I got out of the truck, she straight-up told me that I wasn't gay and that I needed to go back to men. I dated a couple of girls after that, and Ashley was right. We skipped school together as friends from that day forward. We're still friends. Turns out she isn't gay either. She gave me a little boy who calls me Aunt Jesi and the sweetest little girl—blessed with a friendship for life.

Reflection

Unintended pregnancy was my first experience face-to-face with reckless actions having consequences. Consequences far worse than an ATV crash, school suspension, losing friends, or gaining enemies. Worse than any parental punishment or fight. This should have been a huge wake-up call. Far from it, it was just the start of my self-destruction and attachment to external validation. The only difference: a focus on quantity versus quality. No more serious boy-friends. Insecurity drove me to date with no standards. I wonder where I'd be now if I had focused on racing or my studies instead of on the opposite sex. My biggest adversary was me.

5

North Carolina

Starting tenth grade, I was physically recovered but still pretty numb from the inner turmoil that wasn't addressed post-abortion. Pushing it down, I coped by pouring my energy into racing mini quads. Using a mini quad in GNCC youth class hare scramble races wasn't unusual, but it was for me since I had been used to driving a full-size powered quad since age eight. Mini quads, as the name implies, have a lower powered engine. Due to insurance and safety reasons, the series we raced followed manufacturer age guidelines, so I went from a full-sized 450cc quad to a small 90cc mini quad. AND I GAVE HER HELL.

Apart from racing, I recall one serious argument. It was with a girl in my same grade. This girl had had a baby over the previous summer. We weren't close friends, but we were friendly since our whole grade was pretty close. When gossip about my situation emerged, she asked me about it, and we argued in front of our entire geometry class. I remember saying something negative about "kids raising kids" to start the fight that ended our friendship. I said hurtful things to this girl out of my own unaddressed emotions. Seeing her was a painful reminder. I couldn't handle it. I turned my anger towards her and picked a fight.

At the end of tenth grade, when Jodi and I were racing better than ever, something life-changing happened. A tire company offered to sponsor us on the condition that we relocate to North Carolina. Sponsorship included covering entrance fees, travel, and ATV maintenance. My parents were receptive to the proposal because sponsorship meant Jodi and I could keep racing without costing them any more money they didn't have. Races were expensive. Not just the entrance fees for each race but travel, including fuel, hotel,

Jodi and me (left) during our teen years with Dad.

and food. With the GNCC scheduling 13 races a season, it added up quickly. On top of that, there was the ongoing upkeep of the quads—servicing and replacing parts. Plus, after so many of my crazy escapades and self-imposed crises growing up in Canton, we all were ready to start over.

Weighing the pros and cons, Mom and Dad decided we should do it. It would be a big change, but, ultimately, they knew real estate was more affordable in North Carolina than Ohio. The winter weather would be milder, too, which would mean a longer training season, and North Carolina sat roughly equidistant from most of the GNCC race locations, making all of them easier to get to.

Mom announced, "Girls, we want you to chase your dreams, and who knows how far you will go. It will be a big adventure." Mom was dead set on giving us a better life than she'd had. Dad just loved his girls unconditionally, and he showed us that by spoiling us.

I was excited. Hopeful. Optimistic. An opportunity to start over. A new school. A new crowd. I could redefine Jesi by not moving around the block or even to the other side of town but by moving

Racing bestie Cheyanne (left) and me at a GNCC event

to North Carolina! Of course, this also meant saying goodbye to my older sister, Hope. Goodbye to Macy, Ashley, and Lauren. Goodbye to camp and celebrating holidays with my aunts, uncles, and cousins. Goodbye to the home my parents bought shortly before I was introduced to the world. I would be several hundred miles and states from Ohio. Several hundred miles from everything I had known my whole life.

For weeks, I counted the number of sleeps until we moved. With just one sleep left, I walked into the Division of Motor Vehicles to get my first driver's license. At 16, I wasn't nervous. I had been driving in some form or fashion most of my life. I passed on the first try, knowing it was the final hurdle between us and North Carolina. After I slept my last sleep in my childhood Ohio bed, I woke up ready. Grabbing my day-old driver's license and packed bags, I joined Jodi and Mom in the loaded Ford Expedition while Dad stayed in Canton to work. Mom and I took turns driving the seven-and-a-half hours to our sponsor's house in the sparsely populated town of Maiden, only a short 40 minutes northwest of Charlotte, the largest city in North Carolina. In the car, Mom reviewed the plan. She wasn't nervous since we had discussed it many times before, but she said she wanted to ensure we fully understood.

Taking a breath, she began. "I'm staying with you at your sponsor's house for a night or two, then heading back to Ohio. Dad and I will take a few months to settle things and get our new place in North Carolina. Of course, we will still see each other meeting up at the weekend races." Jodi and I were super energized. We couldn't wait to get there and begin this new chapter.

Upon arrival, Jodi and I went on a hunt for our favorite addiction, sweet tea. The obscene amount of sugar they use to make sweet tea is enough to get you wanting more. And at only a dollar a pop, it was a treat our broke teenage asses could afford. In Ohio, McDonald's was the ONLY place to get the sweetest sweet tea. With my fresh driver's license and my sister ready for the ride, we hopped in Mom's car and giddied it up to a McDonald's. We drove 18 miles just to get sweet tea from McDonald's. An hour later, we returned to the house.

Our new host family and Mom asked in unison, "Where did you go?" Innocently, we explained that we had gone to McDonald's for sweet tea. The host family lost it. Apparently, in the South, you can get sweet tea everywhere. *Who knew?*

This was our first lesson on the Southern lifestyle. Even as a kid who extensively traveled to races, I had led a sheltered life. I had never been on an airplane. When we traveled, it was always for the races. Instead of staying in a hotel, we camped at the track. We'd open up the trailer, move our quads outside, and inside blow up air mattresses for sleeping. Our cooking system was a cooler with a grill on top. We made dinner and hung out with our track besties. In the morning, we had breakfast, raced, and headed home while enjoying the gorgeous views and varied terrain out of the truck windows. Because my parents are kid-focused, we enjoyed wholesome kid fun. No stuffy museums or fancy restaurants for us. Starting with that lesson in sweet tea, leaving our protective family cocoon brought a cultural learning curve we never saw coming.

As youth racers in Ohio, we raced only with the boys. At the time, GNCC did not have a girls' youth division like they do today. Racing with the boys, my crowning achievement was the day I made it to the podium and became the first girl on a GNCC youth ATV podium. Pride swelled inside me as I stood beside the boys. I glanced down at my racing bestie, Cheyanne. She was a couple years younger than I was. Not long after my stand on the podium, Cheyanne became the first girl to win a GNCC youth ATV race overall. We were fast and among the only girls in the youth classes during our respective eras. We were a small minority but beginning to carve our sports niche.

Settling into North Carolina, I prepared myself for change. The first was moving to a new level of GNCC series racing, moving out of the youth division and into the Women's Amateur class. The next was adjusting to a new high school. Arriving at my new school, I was so ready to start 11th grade. As excited as I was, right away I encountered challenges. As in Canton, the kids at my new school grew up together. Their cliques were well formed by 11th grade with no room for an outsider like me.

A routine developed. I'd meet a new kid, and they'd ask their first question: "Where are you from?" I'd take a breath and then respond, "A small town in Ohio called Canton, you know, where the Pro Football Hall of Fame is...?" Each time, students gazed at me with puzzled looks, a shoulder shrug, and a change in the conversation. This wasn't done to be mean, but it left me feeling like an outsider. The second question asked was always "What church do you go to?" It was odd to them that I didn't have a church, and I felt the pressure. Being a natural-born rebel, after a while, whenever questions on the subject of religion came up, I doubled down, saying, "We don't have a church. My family has never attended church, and we aren't starting now." That combination of peer pressure and an inner feeling of lack of purpose in my life led me to atheism. It wasn't long before this new kid told everyone who asked simply, "I don't believe in anything," effectively making those pesky questions stop.

The way I spoke was another thing the kids teased me about, calling it a "Yankee accent." This began early, around the second week of school, when I was still a new kid. After a while, the mocking of my speech became super annoying, interfering with my plans to be a better person in North Carolina.

Once, passing between classes in the hallway, I heard someone repeat something I had said in the prior class. They kept repeating the word "coffee" to mock me. I could have let it go, but instead

I quickly turned around, snapping in a sharp tone, "Shut the hell up!"

I made my way to the end of the hall. A short female Spanish teacher from the classroom next door was nearby, within earshot. The teacher grabbed the top of my backpack with one hand and pulled. Her plan was to get my attention to reprimand me for my foul mouth. Without bothering to turn around to see who was grabbing me, I took an aggressive swing at the source of the pulling while thinking, *Don't touch me, bitch.*

Although I didn't make contact, the teacher was upset. She reported me, which resulted in an out-of-school suspension. I sat in the principal's office waiting room, my dreams of reinventing myself into someone calm, sweet, and popular going up in flames.

After that first suspension, word got out. "Don't mess with Jesi. She's a wild one." I quickly found myself hanging with the girls who hung out at parties, got drunk, and smoked cigarettes in the bathroom. It was comfortable and familiar yet miles apart from my previous dreams.

Besides the new school, we lived with a new family: our tire sponsor, his wife, and their two young children. Before moving, I was so preoccupied with the dream of how different and perfect North Carolina life would be that I never thought too deeply about what it might feel like under someone else's roof. Someone we only knew from the racetrack. It felt weird. Showing us around the house, our host family told us to put our things in the elementary-age daughter's bedroom. The girl went to a room nearby. Given how much I cussed, this got me thinking: *This isn't going to go smoothly.* The whole scene was enough to tarnish the shiny newness of our big move.

Jodi and I coped by sticking together and working on getting wheels. "We need a vehicle to escape the school bus and to generally have more freedom!" we complained to our sponsor. He decided to help us out. "Okay, you girls can use our Chevy pickup truck. It's a spare vehicle anyway."

Sitting high in the big truck, it felt so good to have some freedom. Jodi and I cranked the music as I drove her to and from school. Sometimes, we would stop off and do something fun after school. Then, I got greedy. Once I left school in the middle of the day. I didn't see much value in what was going on academically that day and simply didn't want to be there. Plus, I reasoned with myself, *You skipped all the time at Canton South, so what would be the difference here?*

I hopped into the truck and drove away without realizing that the school security guard had spotted me. This landed me in the principal's office again with another out-of-school suspension. Why they had me miss more school for missing school is still a mystery, but regardless, I was in trouble. For my punishment, the sponsor gave me the job of loading and unloading the other sponsored racers' tires for the upcoming race weekend. Pointing to the trailer and the piles of tires, he said, "I don't care how long it takes or how heavy the tires are. You keep going until it's done."

I managed to mostly stay under the radar at school after that until our parents moved to North Carolina three months after we did. They rented a house so we could all live together as a family again. Between school and racing, the weeks flew by. Towards the end of 11th grade, to get in more practice, our sponsor had us doing a local hare scramble racing series called Mideast. I didn't mind. I loved racing outside of GNCC. There was less of a serious approach and more of a party mentality. Sometimes, we camped at the racetrack.

To my naive teenage eyes, my sponsor, a guy in his late thirties with a wife and two young kids, was super cool to spend extra time with us, not minding that we drank and even helping us do it. I believed I knew everything at that age, but I knew nothing about how adults could groom and manipulate kids to meet their selfish desires. When it came to doing things my parents would disapprove of, like drinking alcohol or messing around with boys, our sponsor assured us that what happened on race weekends stayed at the racetrack. My sister, sponsor, and I had an unspoken agreement to keep secrets from our parents.

On the way to a Mideast race where we planned to camp overnight, my sponsor pulled into the liquor store. He bought himself supplies and my favorite liquor, this cinnamon hard candy drink. He handed the bottle to me, and I was ready to indulge. At 16 years old, I had been drinking alcohol since middle school. Back home in Ohio, I made my version of a Kamikaze late at night or early in the morning, sipping off the remnants of drinks from my parents' house parties hosted in our basement bar room. So while I was no stranger to alcohol, I was not super experienced drinking large amounts.

Lying alone on the couch in the camper, I took a sip. It was smooth, so it went down easy. After a few sips, I left the camper for a quick hookup session with a boy I had been flirting with earlier. Reentering the camper, I again grabbed the bottle. There was no reason to drink more; it wasn't a social situation. Yet it tasted good, so I thought, *What the hell.* Plus, getting drunk meant numbing my emotions until I didn't feel anything.

I drank almost half the bottle and threw up in the middle of the night. I woke up with a massive hangover the next day. Feeling poorly from my self-imposed misery, I rode like shit, making a lot of mistakes throughout the race. Lacking focus, I hit a large tree root just right, ripping off my tie-rod on the front end of the quad. That was it. My day ended early. I never owned up to exactly what happened. *Not my fault. That root jumped out in front of me.* That nauseous day became a preview of more to come.

I continued to race, but, thanks to partying, I lost the laser focus I had as a younger kid. Anyone could see that by scanning my results. Yet, it was still fun socially, especially when it was time for the event closest to home, Big Buck, in Union, South Carolina—an early-season race. The Snowshoe Ski Resort race in West Virginia was another one I looked forward to, mainly because it was one big party. My taste for partying and the social aspects of racing outpaced my desire to win.

Before finishing my 11th grade year, I learned that early graduation was an option. Even though I hung out with the party crowd, I still passed my classes and had a good amount of requirements behind me. Never totally feeling at home in my new school and wanting to escape an increasingly uncomfortable situation with my sponsorship, I worked hard to finish high school one semester early. *You can do anything for one more semester,* I convinced myself. In racing, I was set to move into the women's professional division the year I turned 17. My childhood dream was finally coming true. Yet, I was only occasionally showing up for the social aspects of the events while getting lackluster results anyway. I didn't care that graduating early meant losing the tire company sponsorship. I wanted to get out and on my own as fast as possible. Knowing that once I made up my mind about something, there was no talking me out of it, my parents agreed.

Graduating in January, I went straight into the workforce. I was 17. My first job after early graduation was as a hostess at Lone Star Steakhouse. Lone Star Steakhouse was a casual American restaurant chain. I worked in almost every role at that restaurant, from host to server, dishwasher to line cook. To earn even more money, I started collecting waitress jobs. Lone Star, then Sagebrush, and finally the more casual Five Guys Burgers and Fries. I spent everything I made on partying. I stopped GNCC racing shortly after graduating from high school because I had to pay for it myself and it was no longer a priority.

Reflection

How easy it is to conform to what you believe is normal. To revert to what you know rather than change. What I knew was how to be a "good time" girl. That baseline of who I thought I was never changed, so naturally I stuck with it. My plan to change myself into someone better in North Carolina and achieve at a high level in GNCC failed like a fad diet.

6

Cheater

"Cheating on a good person is like throwing away a diamond and picking up a rock."
—*Unknown*

It was during this waitressing phase that I met an important person in my life. I called him Papaya, a nickname I gave to my new boyfriend for no particular reason, but it stuck. An inside joke throughout our relationship and beyond. We met working at the burger place. He was a stunner. Confident at six feet three inches tall with brown hair peeking out from under a backward baseball cap. Best of all, a smile that melts hearts.

After meeting him, Mom said, "He is really easy on the eyes." When Papaya kissed me, my heart jumped like an engine restarting. His strong, protective fingers wrapped tight around mine like a promise I could hold on to forever. *I am all in.* A year older, Papaya possessed bad boy coolness on full display as he drove us everywhere, his car windows fully down while loud, heavy bass rap music blared loud enough for those in neighboring traffic lanes to hear. We felt powerful. Two cocky kids cruising around with attitude while slowly blowing smoke from our cigarettes into the sky, adding to the music's aesthetic. He sold weed on the side, which enhanced his cool factor in many young people's eyes, including mine. Within a month of meeting, we dove headfirst into a three-year roller coaster of a relationship.

Around the same time, Dad and I started arguing more and more. Us arguing was nothing new. Dad and I had always butted heads. Yes, he spoiled me, but at the same time he liked to get under my skin by teasing me or starting an argument. Now out of high school and in a stable relationship, I felt empowered. Plus, Mom was over the road driving a semitruck, so she wasn't there to mediate. One day, a massive disagreement sent me on my way. "Jesi, if you don't want to follow our rules then get out!" Not uttering a word, I packed my stuff and moved in with Papaya at his mom's house. I doubt my dad meant for me to get out, but I left, and no one stopped me.

Living under his mom's roof and eager to get us our place, Papaya secured a higher-paying factory job. He was good at it, and it paid well, especially as he quickly moved into leadership positions. We started going out less and thinking more about our future—a future where we could have careers and someday own our own house.

As for my career, getting orthodontic treatment (for the second time) inspired me. Despite selfish tendencies, I did love to make people smile, and working on teeth seemed like a good way to do it. Tossing ideas around, I posed a question: "Hey Papaya, what do you think about me going to school to be a dental assistant?" Papaya responded, "Jes, what a great idea. I'll back you up so you can do it."

Papaya generously paid for my dental assistant classes, and the office where I got my orthodontic treatment kindly gave me an intern spot. After a month of interning, I secured a regular day job as an orthodontic assistant. The pay was $15 per hour, a decent wage in those days, with advanced training for a long-term career. I was stoked for that job and my future.

Papaya's motivation to pay for my schooling was to get me out of the restaurant business. "Jes, this party atmosphere isn't good for you or us. You have a good day job now. Quit those night jobs and we'll settle down for real."

That didn't happen, though. I kept working part-time in restaurants at night while working in the orthodontic office during the day. I didn't want to give up that life, including making some extra money on the side. We saved enough to settle into an apartment. A routine started. We went to our day jobs. On the nights I had my server job, Papaya stayed home or hung out with his friends. After my serving shift, I stayed out late with other servers or line cooks, often using fake identification to get into the bars. Once in the bars, I'd get ridiculously drunk, flirt, sometimes hook up with guys, and then drive home to Papaya.

They say practice and repetition make things easier to do. Lies are a good example. I don't remember the first time I lied to Papaya, but I do remember one huge lie formed from a million little ones. I entered into a second relationship with one of the guys at work while living with Papaya in the apartment we shared. We had some drunken post-work nights together before he properly asked me out.

The night we were to meet up, I told Papaya, "I'm going out with my girlfriends." He didn't question me. He never did. Possibly out of trust or out of fear, but regardless, the cycle continued. To me, it was playing around, playing until my lies caught up with me and Papaya found out.

One day one of our mutual female restaurant friends asked to temporarily move in. "Can I crash at your place for a few weeks? I'm moving out of state soon and in between apartments. You would be doing me a huge favor." Papaya and I agreed because she was a pretty good friend, and being young ourselves, we knew how it felt to be broke and in between places.

I knew this friend was close to some other girls I partied with from the restaurants. Because of that, she knew about my shady encounters with other guys and how crappy I was to Papaya behind his back, but it didn't worry me. Instead, I thought, *Girls have a code of silence. Of course my secrets are safe.*

I was wrong: it should have worried me. Not everyone tells you exactly what they think of you to your face. In this case, she let out her true feelings when I least expected it and in a way that shocked me. A few days before leaving our house, she waited until I left for work. Then she sat Papaya down and told him everything. Every person I cheated with, every little detail, explaining, "I can't leave without telling you the kind of person Jesi is. She can't be trusted. You deserve to know everything."

The world I knew was about to explode. Blissfully clueless, I came home from work the day she moved out, looking forward to it being just the two of us again. Instead, to my total surprise, they both packed up and left. Apart from my things, such as kitchen supplies, a washer and dryer, towels, and the couch, the apartment was empty. A framed picture of us was left where the bed once was.

Eventually, I found out what happened. I cried for a day and then went to my other man. The affair I was having heated up. I wasn't attached to this second guy, but he told me, "I'm crazy about you." He secretly sought out my parents, asking their permission to marry me.

I went along with it for a little bit. I went as far as looking at houses with him. The art of a good lie is confidence. If people think you are sure of what you are saying, they will believe you. I was not only a good liar but a practiced one. People tended to believe me.

Mostly, I just liked his truck. He even let me use it when he went to Texas for a week for new job training. A girlfriend and I drove that fancy truck 45 minutes from where we lived in Mooresville to pick up a couple of guys I knew from Ohio who were visiting North Carolina.

Still underage, instead of hanging out where they were staying, I told them, "Let's go back to Mooresville to a bar where they will serve us without ID." They agreed, having time to kill and nothing better to do that night.

We drank together for a few hours before I drove them back. At a police checkpoint, one of the officers noticed that the dude in the back seat had an open container. He was so drunk he didn't even think to hide it going through the checkpoint. The police officers signaled us to pull over and get out of the car. I'm not gonna lie to you now. I was a little tipsy. When the officer asked me if I had been drinking, I smiled sweetly. "No, officer, I only had one glass of wine earlier because I'm pregnant." I wasn't pregnant, and I'd had more than one drink. He let us go, but before I left, the police officer privately showed me a photo of his little daughter, quietly saying, "Choose better friends for your little one." I felt bad for a second, then moved on.

Papaya and I were still talking. After a two-month separation, he agreed to give it one more try. As soon as I finally got him to agree to move back in, I coldly ended it with the other guy. We were reunited—back together—and promises were made. Papaya and I refocused our attention on working and saving enough to buy our own house. The housing market was favoring first-time home buyers. We found and bought a cute three-bedroom, two-bath place with a single-car garage at the back of a housing development.

It was a cookie-cutter style of house, except we had a screened-in porch. This was our spot for smoking cigarettes and relaxing with friends. Having our very own place that we owned was good, at least in the beginning. I stopped being so wild, and we did more things together. Now that we had more yard space for toys, we bought dirt bikes, and I returned to riding my four-wheeler.

6. Cheater

My ATV beckoned me from its parked position in our garage. I started racing the GNCC circuit again, returning to my male attention–seeking ways. It was too much of a temptation for my impulsive, 20-year-old self. I began the self-destructive cycle all over again, staying out late at night gallivanting with men. I suspected that Papaya knew what I was doing, but he never confronted me.

One day, we packed our bags. It was time to go to the GNCC race in Kentucky. In another year or so, I will switch to racing dirt bikes but on this day it was all about four wheelers. We drove together in my truck, and Papaya paid for our gas and other expenses. I lived paycheck to paycheck, so I rarely had money on me. Arriving at the racetrack, I carried on as I always did. The difference was that Papaya was watching more closely, knowing my past indiscretions and recent late-night behavior. He was suspicious and—understandably—no longer so trusting. In a state of self-absorbed oblivion, I circulated the field of campers where other racers set up. There was one racer in the "pro row" I was interested in. I went straight there. It didn't take long before I went into that racer's trailer.

Papaya noticed. He left me at that Kentucky racetrack in anger and sadness over my blatant betrayal. I had the car I'd arrived in but didn't have the money to get home.

Seeing no other options, I swallowed my pride and phoned my parents. "Please, send me some money so I can get home!" True to their character, they helped me out. When I finally got home, my things were packed in boxes and placed in our house's garage. Financially, I had no choice but to return to living with my parents. I knew I had gotten what I deserved, but that didn't stop the tears streaming down my face in an all-consuming self-pity. Years of living together, buying a house, and planning a future abruptly ended. I didn't feel cool or special like the guys at the track made me feel. I didn't feel secure or loved the way only Papaya could make me feel. The only thing I felt was sorry for myself.

Reflection

On the outside, I had it all—a good-looking, mature boyfriend; a budding career in orthodontics; and a home—by age 19. Inside, I was wrecked. I wanted to be liked and noticed. I was addicted to male attention for the temporary high and validation it gave me. Seeking out men who took me to high highs along with lower lows. Once I hit a low, meaning rejection or poor treatment from men, I was on the prowl again, chasing those highs.

Maybe if I had communicated my insecurities and desperate need for attention better to Papaya, I wouldn't have cheated, and we would have lasted. After all, we truly did love each other. Instead, I looked elsewhere to meet those needs with disastrous results when communication could have set me free.

7

Bankruptcy

"Don't be afraid of change. You may lose something good, but you'll probably gain something much better."
—social media post, December 2014,
posted between getting Roxanne
and our families' Christmas visit

Between trouble at work, my failed relationship, and financial ruin, the hole I had dug for myself was vast. I was fortunate to have a family willing to take me back. My parents allowed me to move home, like a dog with its tail between its legs, into their spare room in the basement. My sister was less than thrilled to share her space with my wild self, but she had no choice. After several months of denial over my debt and seeing no other option, I filed for bankruptcy to get out of my responsibility for my portion of the house and truck and to dig myself out of accumulated credit card debt. I would be taking a ding on my credit for a few years. Credit wasn't the only thing taking a ding either. Bankruptcy dings your pride, too. I felt shame over my self-inflicted circumstances.

Back at my parents' home, I took in a grim reality. My relationship with a really good guy was over. I had no plan for my future and was officially bankrupt. Taking stock of what I did have, there was my ride-or-die bestie Jessica from the Lone Star days. We were both single, and we grew closer, spending loads of time together, often taking turns staying at each other's places. Jessica became the kind of friend who was, and still is, like family. Along with Jessica, I still had my job at the orthodontist office, and I was still young, so there were a few things going for me, including one solid excuse to keep partying. After all, I was dumped. Partying blurred my reality, keeping me in a foggy detachment.

Jessica (left) and me outside of the hospital two weeks after the accident.

Party girl who loves her high heels.

7. Bankruptcy

Racing a local race for the first time after switching to dirt bikes.

Frequently, I overslept for work due to partying the night before. Showing up to the orthodontist's office late became a habit. It messed up the entire flow with the patients throughout the day. It was a selfish move, yet I was getting away with it, so I kept doing it. My boss, the doctor, was a very laid-back and trusting person. He wasn't the type to get worked up over someone not arriving on time. One day, I rolled in my typical 40 minutes late. This time was different; he noticed. Pulling me aside, he asked me to sign a piece of paper.

The kind doctor said, "Jesi, this paper is your promise not to be late again. If you are, you face immediate termination." Shortly after the paper was signed, he moved me to part-time, replacing me with a more reliable person. Instead of being angry at myself for my lack of commitment to the job, I was mad at my boss, complaining to anyone willing to listen and seething inside: *How could he do this to me?!*

Luckily, I didn't have to scramble to find another job. A few months prior, I had started working part-time in the parts department at a motorcycle dealership. I asked for more hours, and they bumped me up to full-time. This motorcycle shop was great fun with awesome people. Yet it paid less than the orthodontist's office, and I didn't have my shit together enough to stand out for advancement. Work was no longer a career path. It became a place to spin my wheels, to hide out for a while to live in the moment without consideration for my future.

Relationship-wise, I jumped from one superficial relationship to another, opening myself up to an increasing number of lower lows delivered through drunken appraisals. There was one guy in particular who gave me regular degrading feedback. "You look better with glitter on your eyes" and "You need to work out more" were some of his favorites. I started to question myself. Over time, those tiny pokes turned into all-out assaults. After riding four-wheelers all day, he'd say, "You stink. Take a shower" or "You are weak."

His comments left me insecure, so, naturally, to get the highs again, I kept getting after it. Night after night. When he left me feeling empty, I returned to the old routine of seeking validity from other men. I knew nothing about healthy boundaries and relationships then, but I thought I knew everything. I thought I had all of the answers when, in reality, I had none.

The year before my accident, Jessica and I went out to dinner. I started telling Jessica about this guy playing mind games with me. Nothing too terrible, just alternating between leading me on and pushing me away. Seeking revenge, we went by his house together after hanging out late into the night. I'm not sure who thought of this idea, but we egged his driveway—throwing egg after egg in the darkness out of the car window and into the driveway. It was a pretty immature thing to do, but, at the time, our 20-year-old selves thought it was hilarious.

A couple days later, for no damn reason, I decided to again mess with the poor guy who got egged. I texted him something flirty, and he invited me to his place. Feeling mean-spirited, I asked him how he got eggshells in his driveway. I listened to him tell me how he was vandalized. He talked, and I faked an empathetic look while inside taking dark pleasure in the ruse. I became addicted to the chaos. An absolute menace.

This cycle of partying late and sleeping in dragged on. My most self-destructive behaviors set in during the two years before the accident. Alcohol abuse but also prescription medications. Pain pills, usually Percocet or Norco, that my party friends gave me. We would crush the pills, make lines, and snort them in disgusting places like on the lids of toilet tanks.

I told myself: *It's okay. After all, these are prescription medications from a doctor.* Somehow, I bought into the ridiculous myth that prescription drugs were safer for me than illegal ones like marijuana or psilocybin. I thought man-made medicines were better than plants. Abuse is abuse. Regardless of how we justify it.

I was out of control in every aspect of my life. My driving record reflects this. By some miracle, I have no driving-while-intoxicated arrests, although I surely deserved those too. I still get the shivers thinking about the number of times my drunk self got behind the wheel. Once, during those insanity years, I had a near miss in pornography modeling.

My sister's former boyfriend dabbled in photography, having taken some shots of me in my ATV racing jersey. One day I was going into the woods with him for racing photos, and he started talking in an especially warm, friendly voice. He said, "You know, you could make a lot of money in amateur pornography." I rolled my eyes. "I'm serious." Then he surprised me by telling me something even Jodi didn't know. "I work part-time as an amateur porn actor. I promise you, the money is unreal. We could take a few quick photos now, then later you sign some paperwork and that's it. They pay right away, and, trust me, it's totally worth it."

That should have been enough to send me running, but I thought about the fact I had sent naked pictures to guys I'd dated. I was not camera shy when it came to being naked. I was not shy about being naked in general. So, despite my reservations, I took my clothes off in the woods. He snapped a couple of naked pictures. Afterward, it felt too dirty to me. Just thinking about it gave me a queasy feeling. I couldn't bring myself to fill out the paperwork to sell them. I warned my sister, and, eventually, she ended the relationship. I am so proud of her for that. As for me, I'm grateful I didn't grow up in today's era of social media like OnlyFans because I never had a problem taking nude photos. Shoot, a few photos are probably circulating somewhere, and I'll Kim K this thing later in life.

I continued to party and work while competing in GNCC races occasionally, spending my time jumping from relationship to relationship or, more accurately, guy to guy. I got involved with quite a few, including another military guy. Even though we weren't in a committed relationship (because he was married to someone else), we decided to get matching tattoos. The stars on my right side have half a quote, and he has the other half to match. My half is about being loved in spite of being numb. Appropriate, given how easily I gave my body away like I had no feelings. It's also ironic, given my future nerve damage and literal numbness. Stars because we both love our country. He was already in the military, and I was considering it, his involvement piquing my interest.

Our relationship was doomed from the start, but we bonded, and sneaking around added to the excitement. Of course, I hit a new low dating a married man with no concern for the potential consequences. Yet, since I thought of myself as the center of everything, it never occurred to me that I was the other woman in that situation. In my mind, the "other woman" was his wife, not me. Someone to be pitied, sure, but not considered.

Some moments in life that seemed ordinary at the time appear extraordinary in retrospect. My dog Roxanne coming into my life eight months before the accident is one of those moments. At the time, I already had a grown husky dog named Nina. Nina was a wild husky, always running away. I figured a puppy would calm her down. Roxanne was the runt of the litter, a tiny yet healthy and adorable husky with classic blue eyes to accompany her white and black markings. I bought her from someone who got her and changed their mind. When I first saw her, I knew. She was PERFECT. Mom and I were doing yard work two days later. As we filled our small riding lawn mower trailer with dirt it became unstable, tipping over and crushing my sweet little snoozing husky puppy.

We rushed her to our vet. They gave her a couple of oxygen pumps and sent us to the animal emergency room. Rox was dying on us. Her breathing was getting slower. I sped. We finally made it. Holding back tears, Mom and I sat and waited. A couple of hours passed. They finally brought us back.

The vet approached with tears in her eyes. "I'm sorry. Rox only has a 50% chance of making it. We'll know in 24 hours."

I saw her behind the glass, in the puppy oxygen tank, my sweet little girl fighting for her life. I visited her after work for two days.

Fortunately, she had a quick turnaround. I picked her up after work, and she returned home to live her husky life. She's the best.

When Rox was about six months old, Nina got out of her outdoor pen, was hit by a car, and died. From that time forward, it was Rox and me against the world. Roxanne provided and, 10 years later, still provides a daily grounding comfort.

The second extraordinary moment happened when Mom's side of the family visited us. It was a rare Christmastime visit coincidentally (or providentially) planned for just one month before I became paralyzed. The occasion was a Cleveland Browns versus Carolina Panthers football game. The Panthers won 17–13. Growing up with my Ohio family all living within a few miles of one another made us close. Hanging out with my older sister, aunts, uncles, and cousins was pure joy. We took full advantage of our special time together, renting a small party bus to take us to and from the game. Afterward, since it was the holiday season, about 20 of us gathered around our living room piano dressed in our Cleveland Browns and Carolina Panthers football gear, sweatshirts, and flannels. My uncle tipped his Browns baseball cap enough to see the keyboard. Fire roaring in the fireplace, Christmas tree glowing, and lights dim, he played while we sang in unison classic Christmas carols and other special songs, including this soothing Beatles classic: "There will be an answer. Let it be."

Reflection

On the surface, I was the outgoing life of the party—the pretty, tomboyish jokester who made everyone laugh with stories of her outrageous antics. What wasn't visible lay deep down underneath the flamboyant smile and laughing party-girl façade. Someone shallow, dependent, and very out of touch with herself. I had no idea who Jesi even was, and I knew it. It was a depressing thought that led to more partying to make myself feel better. Yet, this was also a time of growth punctuated by a feeling of family love and bonding lingering on long after that magical weekend, strengthening me emotionally when I didn't know I would need it. Another nod from God said that I would be okay.

PART TWO

ACCIDENT

8

Hopeful

"'For I know the thoughts that I think toward you,' says the Lord, 'thoughts of peace and not of evil, to give you a future and a hope.'"
—*Jeremiah 29:11 New King James Version*

A couple of weeks before the accident, I decided to start making better decisions. Baby steps towards adulthood. By then, I had gotten my full-time position back at the orthodontist's office. I was only working one full-time job and taking it more seriously. Finally, I had let go of all of my waitressing jobs. I started consistently showing up on time and truly put myself into my work. While the bouncing around indiscriminately between men did not stop, I began to say "no thank you" to prescription pills most of the time. Daily alcohol use continued, but I went to the gym, lifted weights, and did cardio.

All these positive choices were the result of one future-oriented action. I called the local Air Force recruiter to ask about taking their entrance exam. I started telling myself: *I'm going to be in the Air Force soon. I need to get in shape and clean up my act.* My Air Force plans included returning to school to finish my associate's degree. After that, I promised myself I would continue college as long as it took to achieve an even longer-term goal: becoming an orthodontist.

Inspired by the orthodontist I worked for as an assistant, I was in love with the craft. I marveled at how a tiny piece of metal and some wires completely changed the appearance of an individual's teeth, facial structure, and bite. You could do so much with your teeth! Plus, I loved making people smile and giving them a reason to smile. I didn't always show it, but I've always liked being a helper and had a desire to leave the world a bit better.

Thinking about my most recent decisions, I started feeling

something I hadn't felt for a long time. Hopeful. Of course, the reality is that teeth change more easily than people. To fix me, the Air Force would have to break me down and build me up into something better. What that "something" would be, I didn't know. I just knew I didn't want the life I had. I was ready to start doing better and turn my life around.

The day before the accident, I put on a black dress and heels. I enjoyed wearing high heels. Heels made me feel both sexy and sophisticated. But on that day, the day of Papaya's grandmother's funeral, I dressed up for a different reason. To show respect. I was 22 years old. This grandma was my adopted grandma. The grandma who taught me to make biscuits and gravy when I was 19 years old. The one telling me captivating stories of growing up in Kentucky poverty while I sat with her on the back porch of Papaya's mom's house, mesmerized. You may think that a funeral isn't something that would evoke positive feelings, but on that day, there was a personal moment during the service. As the pastor spoke, I felt this wave of calm wash over me—utter peace from head to toe. In an instant, I knew there was a higher power that I had denied all those years and that a higher power would take Granny to a safe place. Sitting in that church, 24 hours before a life-changing accident I had no way of predicting, I experienced a significant life event. Feeling strong and connected to God for perhaps the first time, I took stock of my life's positive direction. After the funeral, with a grateful heart, I posted this message:

> Because I am beyond blessed with great friends and family, a job, and the opportunity for a better future through education, I can not thank everyone in my life enough for their endless support. I can chase every dream and reach every milestone I set for myself. The good Lord tests my faith and strength daily, proving he is on my side. Thank you all for being part of this adventure we call life.
> —social media post, the day before the accident. January 17, 2015

The last day I walked unassisted, I woke up at my parents' house with a low-grade hangover. A little groggy. Bit of a headache. My penance for being a daily drinker. Drinking alcohol was something I did without thinking about it too much at age 22. It was like mindlessly snacking on a huge bag of chips while watching a movie. I would drink if it was around, and it always was. I was that way with a lot of things. I was not worried about the brain fog or headache.

Experience told me that it would dissipate after breakfast anyway. Young bodies are good in that way.

Out of bed and looking in the bathroom mirror, I checked myself out. As usual, I was dressed casually in jeans and a T-shirt on my thin, petite frame. My reddish-dark brown hair was worn loose, hanging just past my shoulders. A bit of makeup, not much, since that level of effort was generally reserved for nights out. Not too bad. Especially when adding my orthodontic-enhanced toothy smile.

Looking in the mirror that morning, I had a flashback to two days prior. The day I gazed into another mirror, the rearview mirror of my car, watching a cop coming towards me. Dread filled my head as I knew he had looked up my driving record, which already had nine points against it thanks to my lead foot. "Miss, you are so far over the speed limit that I must give you a ticket. As of today, adding this ticket to the points you already have, there are 12 points against your driver's license. I expect you will lose your license for a year. Of course, you can always argue your case in court." *Damn it.* I sigh, pushing the depressing thought out of my mind.

It was a Sunday in January. Everyone in North Carolina knows the winter weather is wildly unpredictable—anywhere from 20 to 70 degrees. That day was a lucky day—a beautiful 60-degree sunny North Carolina winter morning. I had to capitalize on the opportunity to ride my motorized dirt bike. I especially wanted some seat time to prepare for my next race in a few weeks. My male friend loaded my KTM 200 on the trailer for a day of riding. Since I was a tomboy, I commonly hung out with guys, preferring to be outside doing anything fast-paced. We went to a large track about an hour from my parents' house, a motocross track with a loop in the woods. I was having a blast in the woods before hitting a creek bed that washed out my rear tire, slamming the bike and me into the ground quickly. I busted my knee against the rocks. Peeling myself out of the creek bed while shaking off the stinging pain, I kept riding. It took a lot more than one wipeout for me to stop. Speeding through the woods was my happy place. Sweet freedom. We finished early in the afternoon, and I returned home and showered.

A few days earlier, something had happened with my truck—a five-speed '93 Ford Ranger nicknamed Danger Ranger. I might have let it go if I wasn't in denial that my driver's license was about to be taken away. Instead, fixing the truck was a high priority. Contemplating what to do, I weighed my options. I was broke, so taking it in for professional repairs was out. Dad normally was a good option, but we were in our same old pattern of fighting quite a bit. Pride stopped me from asking him. The third best option was someone with whom I had an on-again, off-again relationship. A guy we'll call Gifter. Gifter because he was the one I called when I wanted attention, a bike ride, or gifts. Gifter knew a bit about cars, having worked on them previously.

Gifter always gave me what I wanted, but it wasn't free. The price was investing time in a relationship that wasn't right for him or me. As kind and generous as he was, we weren't good together. We fed off each other's reckless nature, and excessive drinking, abuse of pills, and high-speed adrenaline-pumping cycle rides ensued. Gifter and I had cut ties two months earlier. The breakup took some effort since he was the neighbor's nephew, meaning he visited my neighborhood often, so we still saw each other a lot. Weighing my options between Dad and Gifter, I decided on Gifter. In fact, it was easy to talk myself into it: *I'll call Gifter. He knows more about vehicles than I do, and I know he will make time for me. He's not a bad guy, and when we are together I get whatever I want, princess style. I won't have to deal with Dad, and, most importantly, it won't cost me anything.*

I gave Gifter a call, and he came over. After inspecting the truck, he told me it needed a new head gasket, so I had to ask Dad for help anyway.

When I got home from the backwoods ride on the day of the accident, Gifter called. This didn't surprise me. Reconnecting over the truck had opened the door to bring him back into my life. He asked, "Do you want to go on a motorcycle ride later?" Deep down, I knew that continuing to see him was wrong for both of us, but I would never say no to a motorcycle ride. Plus, I felt I owed him something since he came over and inspected the truck. So, I agreed to go.

That evening, I was wearing my favorite pair of dark, Miss Me brand jeans with rhinestones on the pocket, a new light stone-colored Under Armour two-in-one jacket, and baby blue Nike shoes that the married man had bought me. Gifter picked me up. Looking forward to the ride, I quickly grabbed my jacket and helmet before I walked out of the house with Mom yelling "Be safe!" as the door closed behind me. Of course, we didn't know that that would be the last time I would ever walk through that door.

There is no freer feeling than sitting tall on the back of a sports bike. Sport bikes are performance-oriented motorcycles designed for speed, quick acceleration, and fast turns and braking. Gifter's sports bike was a Yamaha R1, a cool-looking red and white 998 cc bike with three different speed modes. My favorite was A Mode because it had the quickest throttle response with a lot of torque and speed. It was so fast that, in my opinion, the R1 had no business being on the street, only the racetrack. We regularly did 180 miles per hour on the interstate, so fast that it felt like I could peel off at any moment. Adding to the adrenaline rush, I often attempted to drag my knee as a passenger while on an on-ramp, feeding my reckless desires.

I had driven Gifter's sports bike once before this ride and loved it. In fact, I was planning to buy my own sports motorcycle as soon as possible. For this ride, though, I was the passenger. Before getting on, I put on the heavy-duty Shoei helmet Gifter had bought me to protect my noggin. In a flash, we took off.

Saddled up, we decided to do our usual 77-mile route: out of Lincoln County, down to the University of North Carolina (UNC) on Highway 485, to Highway 85, back to Brookshire Boulevard on Highway 85, making a loop into downtown Charlotte before finishing the loop by heading back to Lincoln County up 16. That evening, we stopped near UNC and had dinner at Pho Real Vietnamese restaurant. We both liked pho. Since we lived close to each other and knew each other's families, that naturally was our topic of conversation. As we returned to the bike after dinner, Gifter asked, "Our normal route?" I said, "Yes."

We exited Highway 85 South, sitting at the light to make the left onto Brookshire Boulevard to head into downtown Charlotte, North Carolina, as we had done many times. *A fast-paced routine route that folded right into my lifestyle choices.* We hadn't drunk or done any drugs on this outing, but the aggressive riding was in character.

It was a beautiful night with perfect weather. I was smiling, enjoying the ride. Gifter revved the engine. I heard the roar as we quickly gained speed, accelerating into second gear and getting up to 50 miles an hour within seconds. Green light, and as we turned left toward the city, it happened so fast. A black SUV, coming from the other direction, took an unexpected U-turn right in front of us. The motorcycle didn't have enough time to stop to avoid impact. I closed my eyes and tucked my body into Gifter as we hit the right rear door of the SUV. Everything went black.

9

Jesi May

"Jodi called me and told me what happened. I was in total shock. It simply didn't feel real. I was upset and crying, praying to God that you would be okay. At some point, I dropped to my knees and screamed. I asked if you were dead, getting as much information as possible. Soon after, I went to the bathroom and threw up. I said goodbye to work, then came home and packed."
—Hope, on receiving news of the accident

I don't remember much about the first five days I spent in the Carolinas Medical Center surgical trauma intensive care unit. For much of that time, I lay in a hospital bed in a medication-induced coma. Everything was touch and go. They weren't sure if I was going to make it. I remember bits and pieces, like my hands being tied to the bed. Later, they would tell me everything.

The accident happened at approximately 7:30 p.m. Police determined that both drivers were sober. No alcohol or drug use was suspected. The SUV sustained some damage but was drivable, and, according to the accident report, neither the driver nor the passenger was injured. The motorcycle was totaled. After impact, we both were ejected from the motorcycle, catching air for several feet before slamming on the ground at the edge of the highway. Gifter was in shock and was treated at the hospital for a broken leg.

I broke my back in two places. My chest collapsed. I had punctured lungs and two broken vertebrae. My ribs nicked my spinal cord in the T4 region, just below my breasts, leaving me with a complete spinal cord injury that was high enough to cause severe nerve damage. My legs and a good portion of my core muscles were rendered useless. Topping it off, I had a traumatic brain injury that

71

would ultimately prove chronic—the signature gift of high-impact injuries.

In the immediate aftermath of the accident, the focus was on keeping me alive. My heart stopped twice, and I required resuscitation. My lungs were propped up with tubes and devices to keep me breathing until I was able to do it on my own.

Two days after the accident, still not coherent, I pulled the intubation tube out of my throat. I was feisty. So feisty that they put my hands in mittens so I wouldn't keep pulling the tubes out of my body. I had two thick chest tubes—one on each side—that would be removed after a couple more days and replaced by pigtail chest tubes, which (just as the name implies) are curlicue tubes about the size of a straw. Two on the left side. One on the right. Adding to the tube drama, my oxygen was not stable; the staff struggled to keep my numbers up.

Shut off from the earthly environment while the care team fought to keep me alive, I had an experience in the spiritual realm. I was primed for this experience, having felt spirit at the funeral the day before the accident. While unconscious, I heard and saw a vivid vision of my late grandmother coming to visit me. She was beautiful, surrounded by white light, as if in a bright room. Grandma Boyce was my mother's mother, who passed away when I was eight years old. She presented as a taller, thinner version of my mother, and even though I was too young when she died to have any memories of her, I instantly knew who she was.

Grandma told me, "Jesi May, it's not your time; you can't stay with me, and I can't stay with you. You have things to do and people to get back to." She wouldn't let me stay with her, making it clear that I had to return. It was an overwhelming experience. I felt so peaceful and excited to see Grandma, taking in each word. As the visit continued, I thought, *I will never forget this moment.* It was hard to let her go and leave the magical presence. It felt like pure love. Clinging to each word, I said to myself, *She's right. I must go back. Fulfill my destiny.*

Awakening from my coma, I was so excited that the first thing I did was ask for my mom. I realized I was hooked up to machines and badly hurt, but finding out what had happened to me wasn't my priority. In between gasping for air, I told Mom about Grandma and what I had seen and heard, including how Grandma called me "Jesi May" rather than my legal name, Jesi Michele. In an instant, Mom knew the vision was real, and she was certain that I had died at some point after the accident.

Through wet tears, Mom reminded me that Jesi May was the baby nickname Grandma gave me. Only Grandma and Aunt Lora called me Jesi May. That was so many years earlier I had completely forgotten. Mom elaborated. "Giving nicknames to everyone was her habit, something she did as a sign of endearment." Next, Mom grabbed Dad by the shoulders, looked at him straight in the eyes, and insisted, "John, she died." Dad didn't believe it. "Come on Jacki, there's no way. You're full of it."

They dropped the subject until, one night a couple of weeks after the accident, Dad was reviewing my medical documentation for a supplemental insurance claim. He put the papers down. He walked into the laundry room as white as the sheet my mom was folding. Tears in his eyes, he softly said, "You were right. She died." On the paperwork, he had seen that my heart had stopped not once but twice and that they had given me emergency resuscitation both times I coded. Sometimes, in those early days, remembering that vision of Grandma's message of hope was the only thing keeping me alive as I fought for my life. *Grandma's name for me: Jesi May. Jesi May. Jesi May. Jesi May. I wonder if she called me that because she knew. Jesi may survive. Jesi may thrive. Jesi may become more than she ever dreamed possible.*

Fifteen months after the accident, by sheer luck I was reunited with a nurse on my resuscitation team. She couldn't believe I was still alive, shaking her head and saying, "YOU were the girl with the star tattoo on your side?! The one we had to resuscitate?!" When you are the patient, you don't realize that you died. Life stopped, my existence stopped. I was somewhere between life and death. Most patients don't come back from that experience.

In my case, not only did I come back, but I believe my near-death experience happened so that God could tell me he wasn't done with me yet. He had things for me to do that are bigger than I could wrap my mind around. God gave me grace and hope at that moment and reinforced it the day before my accident, as I attended my ex's grandmother's funeral and felt that peaceful feeling wash over me. These two significant spiritual experiences happened within 24 hours of each other, and I've come to believe God was hugging me in that church the day before the accident, reassuring me that life would be okay. My physical life was saved and my spirit was saved as I instantly morphed from an atheist into a believer. I haven't looked back since. These moments of clarity, faith, and purpose are the greatest gifts. A turning point in my life.

Yet, it was only a tiny seed of faith at first. I knew there was a reason I was alive and that my life had value. I had no idea what my purpose was, though, or what I would do with that knowledge. Then there was my badly broken body, matching how broken I felt emotionally. There were so many inner demons to face from the years of reckless behavior preceding and contributing to the accident. Perhaps, if you didn't know me, I looked a bit angelic, lying stone still sedated in that hospital bed, hooked up to assorted tubes and machines, reveling in the knowledge of my newfound God. But don't be fooled. It was about to get messy. Everybody looks good at the starting line.

10

Numb Me

"It's 2 AM, and I'm in my hospital room. The steady hum of machines continuously pumping me with different fluids is stimulating my mind, keeping me reeling. The curtains are slightly open. The gentle woosh of helicopter blades gets louder and closer as the lights dance across the night sky while it descends to the helipad. I wonder if that person is like me. Did they have a life-changing accident, maybe a spinal cord injury? God, what have I done? How will I live this way? I wish I could sleep."

—*journal entry, January 2015*

My first few days in the hospital were an absolute blur. I don't recall all of it, though I know I saw various family members, including my aunts and uncles. I remember asking if I was dying because my uncle, who hardly gets out of Ohio, had made the trip to see me. Next, several cousins and their families came to visit. And, of course, my parents, my sister Jodi, and my friend Jessica never left my side.

About two days into my hospitalization, I pulled the intubation tube out of my throat. My oxygen was already not stable, and they were trying desperately to get my oxygen numbers up. By the fifth day in intensive care, my oxygen numbers finally stabilized. It appeared that their efforts had worked. *Okay, I'm getting better,* I thought. *I guess I'm going to live.* My doctors, optimistic that the 24-hour trend would continue, moved me into the progressive unit.

Shortly after I settled into my new hospital room, the unexpected happened. I reached a critical state again, struggling to breathe. It felt like an elephant was sitting on my chest. After 12 hours of me gasping for air in the progressive unit, the looks of worry on everyone's faces communicated more than words ever

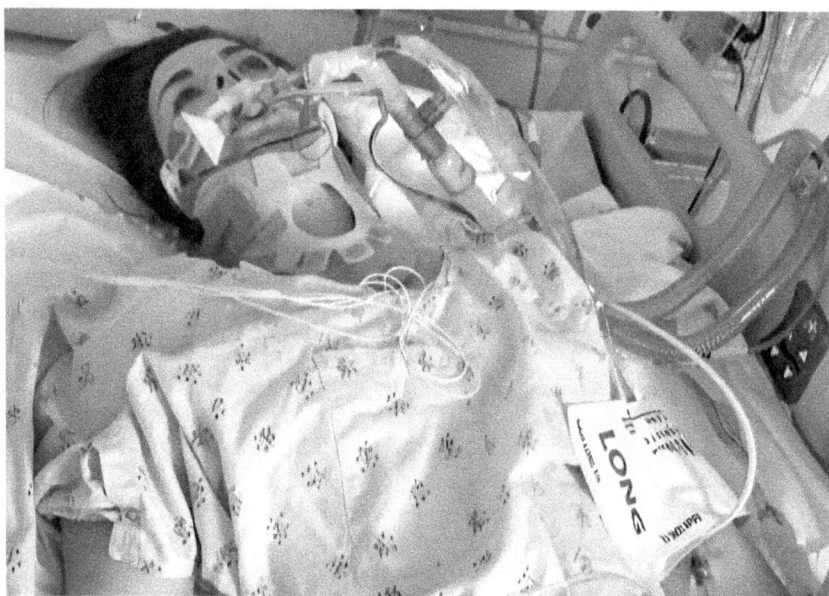

In a medically induced coma hours after the accident.

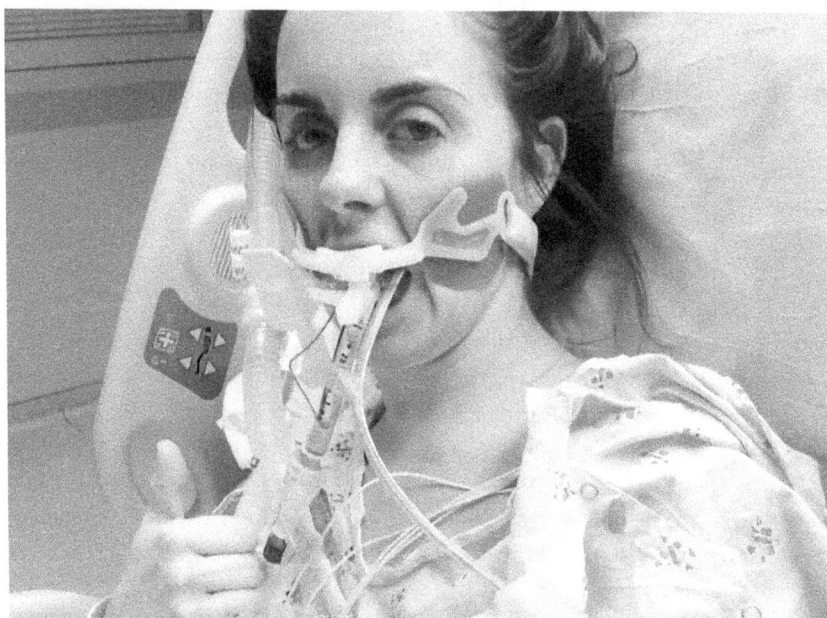

Breathing through a tube: my worst nightmare come true.

could. A medical team gathered, swiftly wheeling me back into surgical trauma intensive care. Next, they immobilized me with straps before inserting into my throat while I was awake the same size tube I had pulled out a few days earlier. I still have nightmares about that moment today; it was traumatic. Lying on the hospital bed with tears running down my face while a tube was being forced down my throat, like some sick scene from the *Saw* movies. Having that tube down my throat was the lowest point of my entire hospital stay.

Lots of friends were in and out. The main visitor activity was encouraging me to blow into a plastic cylinder—I needed to exercise my lungs—but I couldn't and wouldn't. A tracheotomy was needed. A hole cut into my throat to help with breathing until I healed up enough to do it on my own. The thought of looking like an old smoker who had a butthole-looking scar on their neck scared the crap out of me. I fought the nurses, doctors, family, friends, and everyone who tried to convince me it was the way to go.

When I refused to give in, suctioning was offered as a last-ditch effort. Suctioning involved a tube being shoved up my nose and into my lungs. I agreed. Anything to avoid the butthole scar. The last thing I said to the doctor ordering this procedure to insert the suctioning tube was, "You better fucking numb me." I did not want a horror movie repeat. The doctor laughed and said, "Oh, we'll fucking numb you." Shortly after the numbing agent was applied, in went the tube. I choked slightly on the tube even with the numbing agent. After the suctioning, I breathed a bit better at first, but it didn't take long for labored breathing to resume.

Later that same day, my friend Jesse from the motorcycle parts dealership where I used to work came to visit. Jesse is a straight shooter and always my voice of reason; we grew close when we worked together. I explained to Jesse about my problems with breathing, being suctioned through my nose five times in one 12-hour shift, and wanting to progress but not wanting a butthole on my neck.

He stopped me mid-sentence. "Bitch, just get the fucking trach." That made me laugh a little. Then he got serious and broke it down for me. "In life, you must do whatever it takes to get where you want to go. You need this tracheotomy so you can move on to dealing with your spinal cord injury. It's not a choice. All you are doing is delaying your independence."

Part Two—Accident

I thought about Jesse's words and decided he had a point. The next day, when my doctor entered the room, I said, "OK, trach me." Within 30 minutes, the team organized in my hospital room ready to do the procedure. Lights out. I woke up with a "size eight" hole in my neck and a tube coming out of my stomach that was sealed with a peg when not in use. Essentially there were two new holes in my body.

The irony is that today, I don't even notice the scars, and yet I almost let fear stop me from taking action that would ultimately improve my quality of life.

After the tracheotomy, I was voiceless for the second time since waking up from the coma. The first time was when I had the intubation tube shoved down my throat. The difference the second time was that by then my care team knew my talkative personality, so the nurses were probably stoked, and my parents were over the moon. Sadly for everyone else, the silent phase only lasted long enough for me to see the hole and realize it wasn't such a big deal. Vanity about my looks nearly cost me my life. Breathing easier, I was able to leave the intensive care unit.

It was between day two and day four at the hospital that I discovered I was paralyzed. I mean, yes, I was told I had a spinal cord injury as soon as I came out of the coma. Still, I hadn't yet grasped that my spinal cord injury meant paralysis. I wish I could tell you there was a dramatic moment when they broke the news. Maybe some melancholy music or violins playing in the background. Friends weeping at the bedside.

Instead, it happened when I woke up to a nurse between my legs catheterizing me. "What are you doing?" I asked. I saw her working in my genital area, but I couldn't feel anything. She said, "Oh, honey. You have a T4 spinal cord injury. I'm catheterizing you." I still didn't understand, so I replied, "Yeah, okay, so why can't I just use the bathroom?" She had no response to my question. My eyes followed her as she walked out of my room, no doubt more than a little freaked out by my ignorance.

Mind racing, as soon as the nurse exited, I grabbed my tablet and searched "spinal cord injury." Scary words jumped off the screen. *Paralyzed. Wheelchair. Disabled. Numb. Chronic Pain.* Seeing the word *incontinent*, I contemplated one terrifying question after another. *Is that why I needed a catheter? I can't walk AND I can't go to the bathroom like a normal person?! What about sex?! If I couldn't feel her putting a tube up me then that does that mean I won't ever get vaginally aroused or orgasm?!!* It was a lot to absorb. I quickly touched myself. There was no sensation. It felt especially devastating to learn I had no sensation in my genitals. I believed my genitals equaled my worth. I valued my body parts more than my internal being. My view of myself was as shallow as a kiddie pool. It was a lot to absorb. Shock and disbelief at the same time quickened my breath as tears formed in my eyes.

Emotions came in waves. Waves like the angry one crashing down after my first transfer back to the intensive care unit. An occupational therapist visited. She entered my room, announcing in her cheery voice, "Today we are going to try to put socks on." She explained that the first step was for me to grab my leg. So I grabbed it. My calf felt cold, like a piece of meat you just grabbed from the fridge. I couldn't feel my hand on it. Throwing my leg back down, I screamed, "What do you mean I have to put socks on?! Get out of my room! We aren't doing this today!" Then a wave of sadness landed softer in whispered thoughts: *I am the injured party. I am the victim. I'm numb from the chest down. Leave me alone.* As I wrestled with the gravity of my condition, there was tangible hope for recovery.

Earlier on, when I was still unconscious before the surgeon fused my spine, my parents were asked, as my next of kin, whether they wanted to enroll me in a clinical trial to help partially heal the paralysis. It was described as a Band-Aid for your spinal cord. The mice from the trial had positive outcomes, giving much hope for the human side.

The crazy part of this opportunity was that only one other human in the world had undergone the procedure so far. Worried, my mother asked the neurosurgeon if having the procedure would impact my walking again. He replied, "Actually, this is her only chance at recovery." That statement made their decision easy. Wanting to help in any way possible, my parents agreed to the procedure, which set the wheels in motion for it to happen. I was told about it after coming out of the coma.

The spinal fusion and trial implant surgery took place at the same hospital two days after the accident as soon as I was medically stable enough to survive surgery. While fusing my spine, the neurosurgeon cut open my spinal cord. Next came irrigation of the cord to prevent the formation of scar tissue and insertion of the small neuro scaffold, about the size of a grain of rice and similar in appearance to a cotton roll you'd see at the dentist. The aim was to reconnect the disconnect within the spinal cord, allowing a nerve to grow through. Once one nerve grew, the thinking went, another could grow off of it, rebuilding pathways from the part of my body above the injury to the part below.

When faced with paralysis, any morsel of hope is something to cling to—tightly. On my social media page, friends and family encouraged me to work hard. They said things like "Put in the work and surely one day you will walk" or "You are young and healthy. You will bounce back soon." Especially since I'd had the experimental surgery, I clung to those comments, steeling myself with resolve. *This paralysis can be beat. I can do it. Sensation will return.* My implant surgery offered hope and motivated me to recover as I wrestled with the gravity of my condition.

Once I finally worked through enough of the shock and denial to fully grasp the extent of my injuries, I became desperate to find more answers. As any millennial would do, I turned to social media. I joined every spinal cord injury support group I could find. Accepted into the largest group, I asked one simple question: "I was in a motorcycle accident and just found out I'm a T4 Paraplegic. I'm 22 years old. What will the rest of my life look like?"

Hundreds of comments came flooding in along with glimmers of hope. Dozens of people with paralysis took the time to let me know my life wasn't over. People posted photographs of themselves doing sports; working jobs; and being with their partners, children, and extended families. This was the proof I needed that a full life after paralysis is possible. My eyes took in the comforting images. Evidence that just because I was in shock and angry then I might not always feel that way. I clung to these messages during the days and weeks that followed when I was confronted daily with the brutal realities of having a spinal cord injury.

While staying in my hospital room for three weeks before being transferred to in-patient rehabilitation, I connected with the first person who received the procedure—known in medical circles simply as Patient One. I can't quite remember how I found him, but he gave me a lot of ambition for recovery in those early days. In fact, instead of accepting paralysis, we believed we both would walk again, which wasn't hard to do since an onslaught of media attention was producing reports like this one, written by Rebecca Robbins in August 2015 for STAT:

> Stracham, a 23-year-old orthodontist's assistant from North Carolina, is just the second patient in the world to try an experimental device that is implanted in an injured spinal cord in hopes of preserving functioning nerve cells and improving recovery from paralysis.... She only learned after she woke up in a hospital bed in Charlotte, N.C., that doctors had implanted into her damaged spinal cord a small, porous, biodegradable cylinder that the company calls a neuro-spinal scaffold. The device is designed to reduce damage by providing a physical substrate for viable nerve cells to cling onto and grow through, the way soil provides support for the tendrils of a growing seed.

While in the hospital, between visitors and FaceTime dates with Patient One, I spent a lot of time thinking about my past: growing up in Canton, Ohio, crazy times with friends, my years racing off-road. Relationships I'd had, including the broken ones. My choices. Then I thought about my present. My newfound relationship with God through near-death experience, or as I called it, my between-life-and-death experience, my experimental surgery and conviction to walk again, physical pain and shock, and my uncertain future. In some ways, I felt so messed up. Life was turned upside down. I had a long battle to face and was still wrapping my head around how life would be different. Atop my to-do list was saying goodbye to the Air Force dream.

Looking forward, I could see opportunity and a chance to do better. One of those opportunities was finding out that my speeding ticket, received two days before the accident, had been excused. A moment of grace granted by the judge after hearing about my paralysis. Plus, no doubt he bought into the common misconception that paralyzed people can't drive. *What's the point of taking a license away from someone who will never use it?* Learning that my license was safe, I took a deep sigh of relief.

Another positive was a growing sense that I was part of a whole new community. The Disabled Community. I suddenly had a new purpose. Purpose as a participant in the clinical trial and purpose in the challenge of figuring out how to live in a badly damaged body.

Part Two—Accident

I was blessed with a talkative, outgoing personality for better and sometimes for worse. Being friends with me means never having to wonder what I am thinking. My brain injury amplified this trait. As anybody born in the early 1990s knows, technology-wise, we are the generation that benefited from the best of both worlds. We're old enough to have grown up without a screen in front of our faces constantly but young enough to have the advantage and ease of the internet for access to information and worldwide social connections from our teenage years on. By the year of my accident, I had a cell phone. I had a tablet. These become my hospital lifelines to the outside world. Even with a tube shoved down my throat, unable to speak, I could speak online. I could post thoughts and feelings. I could read about the experiences of other people with spinal cord injuries.

Patient One and I shared a worldwide platform that got us noticed, and we both felt an almost immediate romantic spark, stoked with late FaceTime dates in the hospital. This connection restored hope early on. In addition to his social and emotional support, Patient One fed me information about innovative tools like electric stimulation wearable therapy shorts and KAFO leg braces. He told me just what to do for my next steps to maintain optimal physical functioning. People in the online community taught me how to manage the social media attention generated by the clinical trials by starting my own branded business website (jesistracham. com) and making regular posts. This gave me much-needed mental focus and a purposeful way to pass the time.

Although one Twitter reporter called my tweets about being Patient Two "chirpy and upbeat," inside I felt nothing—these were fake it 'til you make it moments. One journalist reported stocks connected to the cutting-edge spinal cord implant rising and falling according to my breezy tweets about sensations in my body. I didn't know it then, but my parents gave me a great gift by signing me up for clinical trials. I had a purpose early on to connect with a larger community while at the same time growing a habit and skill set for sharing on social media. A small platform blossomed—a platform leading to so many other future opportunities from making new friends in the wheel community to finding paraplegic support groups. Social media was my outlet. It quickly became my journal, but instead of pouring my heart out on paper I exposed myself to the masses taking comfort in the knowledge I wasn't alone.

I want to note that while I had an awesome care team overall during that initial hospital stay, it wasn't always perfect. I can't sugar-coat the experience because that isn't fair to readers who have had to endure long hospital stays or to their loved ones who had to step up and fill in the gaps when there was neglect. I remember one time over a weekend shift when I had shit myself. It was a complete blow-out. I hit the call light and was told someone was on the way. An hour went by. I called my aunt in Ohio and told her what was going on. She called the hospital and demanded that someone come in. Another hour went by, and Jessica got there. Still, no one came. Jessica went into the hall and asked, "What the heck is going on?" The next thing we knew, the nursing assistant said, "It's my last night. Sorry." For three hours, I sat in my shit. Finally, Jessica lost it: "I don't give a fuck if it's your last night. You let her sit in her shit for three hours!"

In addition to Jessica, the entire GNCC community came together most magnificently. There was this particular photographer who watched us all grow up. She is a boss woman in a man's world. So much so that I'm not surprised she was the one who started the Team Jesi initiative, getting permission from my parents mere days into my hospital stay. Team Jesi included a GoFundMe campaign to which so many people generously donated. The fundraiser bought me a lift and higher toilets. Plus, it paid for driver's education classes and adaptive hand controls for my car. After all, the judge had let me keep my license and I was ready to roll. For solidarity, Team Jesi bracelets and T-shirts were made.

Reflection

It's cool to see a family member or someone I knew who still has that bracelet as a memento of their care, connection, and tangible support in my time of need. I could go on and tell more stories, but the essential takeaway is to make those hospital visits to friends, coworkers, and family. Show support and be an advocate. They need you. It's time well spent and helps fight any neglect that may happen. The abundance of love in our life is sometimes out of our view.

PART THREE

POST-ACCIDENT

11

Rehab

"Things were pretty scary a few weeks ago, but I got to live to tell about it. The Lord works in mysterious ways, and every day, he gives me the strength to keep on. I roll (because I cannot walk anymore) with my head high. Fighting daily. #theroadtorecovery #para #paralyzed #becauseican"
—*social media post, February 2015*

I moved to the rehabilitation side of the hospital for a three-and-a-half-week stay, and some energy returned. Life got rolling in that rehab unit. Thanks to Jessica's mom, I had my hair washed in my hospital room sink for the first time in weeks before going to rehab. I felt like a girl again, and I even tackled putting on socks for the first time. Thanks to Jessica, I continued to have a regular, friendly visitor—the same Jessica who hiked mountain trails and smashed eggs in my enemy's driveway. When the accident happened, she was the person who drove over an hour and a half to the hospital after work every single day up until I was transferred to the rehabilitation hospital. "Bulldog" was my mom's name for Jessica then, and she still calls her that now whenever she fondly remembers how she stuck up for me in the hospital. After I moved to rehab, Jessica and my parents could cut their hospital visits back from daily to a few times a week.

Thinking about Jessica's level of commitment to me during my time of need, I'm reminded how we often get so caught up in our problems that we don't recognize how much value someone adds to our lives. Jessica is this person. I was very unappreciative of her in the early days after my injury. She called me out on it, and we didn't talk for a while, but we got through it. Eventually we found paved greenways where I could ride my wheels while she walked. We took many road trips together exploring the country. Having her there helped me move forward. She has a family today, including a beautiful little girl I get to watch grow up.

My first turning point towards feeling better at the rehabilitation center came when my breathing was back to normal and they were planning to remove my tracheotomy tube. This boosted my morale. I even felt good enough to go to the main hospital's cafe with my physical therapist for a milkshake to celebrate. After physical therapy, my doctor came into my room. He slowly removed the tracheotomy tube from my neck and took the peg out of my stomach. Then my doctor, nurse, physical therapist, and I all watched with shock as the milkshake I had drunk earlier started to flow with force out of the hole in my belly. Of course, I remembered drinking the milkshake, but it had never occurred to me that it would come spurting out of the gaping hole after removal of the peg tube. We all laughed hard at the bizarre scene of this rancid-smelling milkshake explosion, creating a huge stink and mess simultaneously. That's what carried me through many of those hospital and rehabilitation days, finding laughter even in the struggle. It's what still carries me through today. We laugh and then laugh some more at the disgusting mess. Sometimes, that's all you can do. Today, my physical therapist from rehab still works at Carolina Rehabilitation Center. Now and then, I see her, and we still laugh about it. What seemed so difficult then has become a surprisingly fond memory.

It turns out that an open hole causes more problems than allowing milkshakes to forcibly exit. The one in my stomach dashed my dreams of getting in the pool, which was one of my big goals for rehab. No open wounds in the pool. It wasn't that I was such an avid or strong swimmer before the accident, but getting paralyzed from the waist down makes you feel heavy. I longed to feel lighter in water and experiment with what my body could do in the pool. Later on, when I returned for round two of in-patient therapy, I tried again to get in, but I had a burn on the top of my shoulder from using a heating pad. Once again, an open sore meant no pool time. Disappointed, I turned my focus to what I could do.

The point of being in the rehabilitation unit was for me to figure out the basics of living in my crazy, damaged body. One of my first tasks was learning to transfer from my bed using a slide board device. A slide board is a long, flat board that is an adaptive tool. The idea is to start with the board, and eventually, once you build up enough strength, you can transfer without it. I also learned wheel skills like transferring from chair to bed, doing a wheelie, and showering myself. We even started working on the floor transfer, which I could not conquer.

As for wheel skills, I was issued a copy paste quickie wheelchair. I call it "copy paste" because chairs covered by insurance are all basically templated chairs. A cookie-cutter variety commonly sized a few inches too big to accommodate expected future weight gain. I didn't know anything about wheelchairs. Everything was new to me. Rolling out of rehab, I had no idea how to maintain my wheelchair or learn about other—better—wheelchair options, including how to pay for them. All of that I would learn in the future from wheel friends. Today I have a lightweight Box brand wheelchair customized to my body and movement preferences with suspension in the back and the casters to help absorb the force of the push. It rolls a lot faster. It's more agile and maneuvers better than an insurance chair. Another way wheeled life starts out hard but gets easier over time.

One day at the rehabilitation center, a young, paralyzed woman a couple of years older than me came to visit. She had an injury level similar to mine, worked full-time, had a partner, and competed in water skiing. This simple visit, organized through rehab, gave me my first glimpse of hope that everything would be all right. The visit was so impactful that I decided that when I was released I would continue to visit the rehabilitation center to mentor the newly injured. I kept this promise to myself and still do it today, almost a decade later. You are never alone in your struggle. Someone has lived through something similar to your struggle before you. And someone will go through something similar to your struggle after you. Peer support gave me hope, the best kind of medicine.

The first super emotionally challenging obstacle to face and learn at rehab is how to be independent when using the bathroom. Like a toddler, I had to relearn how to use the bathroom. This was harder than I ever imagined. Something as basic as going to the bathroom became an entire process. I could no longer control it, which was also a little discouraging, but, being sassy, I made the best of the shitty situation. Pun intended. With a lot of spinal cord injuries, you can get something called neurogenic bowel and bladder. It's a fancy way of saying a bowel and bladder you can't control. It affects everyone differently.

For me, a neurogenic bathroom function looked like no bowel or bladder control and having a very, very spastic bladder. Because of this, I had to learn how to use a catheter to drain my bladder and get on a bowel program for my bowels, training them to be as consistent as possible. Learning this practice was super intense and time-consuming. Lucky for me, back then I didn't know it would be another five years before my body settled down enough to gain back a bit of sensation and then a little more around the nine-year post-injury marker. The yearslong struggle of learning how to care for myself with an uncooperative body gave me a strength I don't believe I would have found on my own.

All of this was, of course, new to me. Once, a nurse came into my room. Her fingers reeked of cigarettes. She only worked with me for a bowel program once because I couldn't handle the thought of her cigarette finger going up my butt. It's funny because I smoked cigarettes before I got paralyzed, but having been in the hospital for so long without smoking, I realized I didn't need them. Deciding to never smoke cigarettes again was an easy decision. As easy as requesting that the nurse not be allowed back in my room. I sure hope it didn't hurt her feelings, but ma'am, I don't want your cigarette finger up my butt, thank you very much.

Most of the time, with a spinal cord injury, you have to manually evacuate your bowels by putting on a glove, lubing your finger, and using your finger to make circles in your rectum to help the bowels evacuate. In the beginning, they taught me to use suppositories to help move the bowels. Still, the weird mucus residue left behind left me skipping the suppository part, leaving me to finger blast my butthole, as I called it. Later in the injury, I would be introduced to Navina trans-anal irrigation. This consists of using warm, drinkable water with a digital device to flush the bowels, ideally to the bend in the lower intestine. For me it has been an easier and faster approach when it comes to bowel management.

After three and a half weeks of learning toileting, dressing, transfers, basic wheelchair, and other life skills, my insurance allowance ran dry. I was discharged. Not because I was ready but because that's how the system works. First, you get yourself paralyzed. Second, the insurance company plugs your diagnosis into their computer system. Out pops the cold and calculated number of days statisticians have determined it takes you to learn basic skills to be independent at home. Of course, I'm no expert, and others may have had different experiences, but this is my perception and my story. My time was up; ready or not, I was released to try to figure out the rest on my own.

Freshly discharged, I wheeled through the doors of my parents' home for the first time with a urinary tract infection. I was on an antibiotic plus six other prescription medications. Immediately struggling, I started drinking alcohol excessively, peeing myself a lot and emotionally unhinged. It was a horrifying, scary experience to be dropped off at home without the physical skills to cope.

I remember having several bowel accidents my first week. At the time, I was camping out in my parents' living room, so every time it happened, the entire house smelled. While my parents were working, the neighbor came to help me. The neighbor who was related to the guy who was in the accident with me. *What can I say? Small town.* She helped me wipe my butt, change clothes, etc. The weekend rolled around, and my uncle and his wife came to town. I had been pooping nonstop, and the smell was super intense. Knowing something was wrong with me and that everyone had been drinking, we called an ambulance, and my mom rode with me back to the hospital so I could be checked out.

They wasted no time admitting me and diagnosing me with C. diff, a nasty infection in my intestines that caused my bowels to flow constantly. C. diff can occur with the antibiotics used for a urinary tract infection (UTI), which I had been getting nonstop since the accident. Already pumped up with antibiotics for my UTIs, I had to be put on yet another antibiotic—intravenously—for the C. diff and was hospitalized for a week. My independence regressed significantly due to the strength I lost during that time. Besides that, three and a half weeks hadn't been long enough in rehab. I had a long way to go physically, mentally, and spiritually. My doctors, family members, and other caring providers argued their cases, too, for my lack of readiness to be in a home setting. I got very lucky. My insurance approved three more weeks, and I was sent back to inpatient rehabilitation.

I got back into rehab and was so grateful. After being home for a week, I realized I needed to improve my transfers and toilet mobility to be independent. Gratitude for being gifted with more rehabilitation left me empathetic to the unlucky ones. To live life to its fullest, you must first be able to get yourself to the toilet, transfer to a car, and pick yourself up off the floor when you fall. All of this takes time and training, preferably from other wheelchair users. Yet, this scenario of being discharged before mastering independence is the reality for thousands every year.

During my second round of rehab, my treat on Sundays after an intense week of work was sneaking out of in-patient rehab to driver's ed, where I got to spend six to eight hours learning how to drive with hand controls. Technically, this wasn't allowed. I pulled it off thanks to an understanding nurse and my dad, who picked me up. Having accident insurance through my job as an orthodontist assistant was an absolute blessing. I received enough money from insurance to buy a vehicle, which my parents picked up for me while I was in the hospital.

I loved my diesel-fueled Volkswagen Jetta. Since I knew I needed to learn to drive, I quickly looked up driving schools for people with disabilities. I found an adaptive-friendly driving school in Charlotte—A1 Driving School—and enrolled. The owner and my adaptive driving instructor was well known in the Charlotte area. He stood out, wearing large gold chains around his neck and plush tracksuits. We were on the same page. I would complete driver's ed quickly so I could install the hand controls in my car. We spent hours together on Sundays, and he patiently retaught me how to drive.

One time, we took a break at the outlet mall. It had been a while since I'd left the rehab facility, so I knew I was gonna need to use a catheter to drain my bladder soon. I rolled myself into the large multi-stall mall bathroom. This was my first time using a catheter in public independently, so there was nothing fast about it. I have no idea how much time passed, but it was enough time for a random woman to knock on the door and say that the man outside wanted her to check to see if I was okay. I had been struggling for a hot minute to get my pants back up while in my wheelchair. I ask her to help me pull up my pants. Another new thing. Asking a total stranger to help me do something so personal.

My driving instructor and I got along great. He had such good energy. He was kind enough to ask me about things I liked. Driving the car with my friendly instructor by my side and my wheelchair tucked in the trunk of the car, I felt a sense of normalcy that I hadn't had since the accident. When I mentioned my favorite burger place and how long it had been since I had one, my instructor took me there at the first possible opportunity. On my first day behind the wheel, while pulling back into the parking lot after a day of practice driving, I went to hit the brakes and instead hit the gas, sending us heading straight for a moving truck. An expert in his field, my instructor quickly responded, hitting the instructor brake on the passenger side to prevent disaster. That was the last time I ever did that. I learned my lesson quickly.

My nurse knew about my sneaking out. We pinky promised not to tell anyone. She kindly put in extra effort by giving me the toileting and medication supplies required for each outing. I justified the infraction to my nurse this way. I'd already spent one week at home. I knew what didn't work. I needed to drive for my quality of life and sanity.

That pinky promise played a massive role in me becoming as independent as I am today. Receiving driver's education in the in-patient setting was a game changer because driving is where I feel the most normal. Even in the best facilities, healthcare "systems" are just that—systems—with a one-size-fits-all approach to patient care. That's often not realistic. I was lucky to have an understanding nurse, but I'm also proud that I took action to customize my rehab experience for my needs.

During my rehabilitation stay and one of Jessica's visits, I wanted to show her the wheel skills I'd been learning. I planned to show her a wheelie. Before we left my room, I flipped the anti-tippers on the back of my chair to pop a wheelie. I started my wheelie but instead of raising my wheel and landing gently, I flipped backward in the hallway, crashing to the ground causing a lot of paperwork and a slight headache for the nursing staff. By that point, they were probably ready for their rowdy patient to leave.

What I didn't consider while learning how to drive or wheeling around the rehabilitation center was that somebody else was putting my wheelchair in the car and the rehabilitation center was barrier-free. These were challenges I had not yet faced. Yet, my driving was on point, discharge papers were signed, and I was ready to hit the ground rolling.

12

Romance on Wheels

After my final rehabilitation center discharge, I spent several months traveling. Traveling because driving kept me in constant motion, didn't let the dust settle under my wheels. I knew that eventually I would need to rebuild my life in one place, return to work, pay the bills, etc., but I wanted to be on the move.

Settling into my parents' home, where my struggles would be exposed and I would be forced to look into my loved ones' sad eyes, could wait. Plus, I had an agenda and exciting plans.

The very first weekend post-discharge, I was off to participate in a GNCC race where I rode side by side as a passenger thanks again to the support of the GNCC community. The next weekend, I was on a flight to Boston, Massachusetts, to meet with Patient One. Afterward, it was windshield time driving to and from races before flying again in July to be with Patient One for a month-long stay.

Patient One in the clinical trials is a natural daredevil like me. He loves to be active and is into outdoor adventure sports. Paralyzed while attempting a backflip on a dirt bike, Patient One is hard-working, attractive, and a few years older than me. Our time together was short, only six months, but, true to our nature, it was fast-paced.

Adding to the budding attraction was the excitement surrounding being patient number one and two in a clinical trial with so much promise. From the second week I was in the ICU, we shared Face-Time dates late into the night. We leaned on each other hard during that time. I fell unconditionally in love with him. Being freshly paralyzed and 22 years old, I was still immature and learning my way. Planning a future with someone learning their way may not have been the most constructive, but Patient One taught me a lot about

Top and bottom: Racing GNCC in my Polaris ACE.

not letting the injury get the best of me. His positive mindset helped me in so many ways.

After weeks of talking via FaceTime in my hospital room, Patient One and I, supported by an investor in the clinical trial and the media they engaged to spotlight us, met in Boston for our first in-person meeting. To get there, I flew from Charlotte to Boston. It was my first flight since the accident and the third time I had been on an airplane. The first was when Mom took us on holiday to celebrate our high school graduation, and the second was when I flew back to my hometown in Ohio just months before the accident.

Flying as a wheelchair user for the first time and generally being an inexperienced flyer, I was terrified. I was not sure what to expect. The aisle chair transfer was a little rough, but once I figured it out, it went a bit more smoothly, but honestly the whole experience was a struggle. Injuries from the accident affected my entire body, not just my ability to walk. My new normal involved nerve pain, headaches, and occasional involuntary muscle rhythmic contractions known as spasms.

Adaptive hand control set up with split front and rear brake and a vertical twist throttle.

Part Three—Post-Accident

It was a short in-person visit but enough for romantic sparks to fly. While in Boston, we sat in accessible seating to watch the Boston Marathon. There was a deafening roar as the crowds cheered the runners passing by. It was rainy, chilly, thrilling, and exciting. It was something I would never have experienced without the accident. Next, we attended a fundraiser dinner just for us, which was also organized by the investor in the clinical trial. The fundraiser successfully covered some of our post-accident therapies, including the wearable therapy stimulation shorts I still sleep in today. Shorts that improve muscle mass, leg circulation, and the overall appearance of my legs. Early on, I knew I didn't want bony, paralyzed-looking legs. I've never let go of that, and I stay consistent in achieving it.

Throughout our brief visit, it was clear Patient One understood me in a way others could not. Especially my angry outbursts. Outbursts unfairly directed at him. I was like a pot of boiling water needing to let out steam. Scalding hot unresolved anger over the accident, frustration with so many new physical challenges and also because of my traumatic brain injury. He handled it well during that trip. He empathized as only someone who had been in a similar situation a year prior could. It was impossible not to fall hard for this kind man while my emotions spiraled out of control.

While we were in Boston, he made me pop over to the bed from my wheelchair instead of using the board I had been using. That was Patient One, staying positive and playing to my competitive nature. At one point, I accidentally broke the shower head in a hotel room, shooting water everywhere—one crazy mishap after another. We were ushered all around Boston by our hosts, photo op after photo op. He flew back to Charlotte with me after that trip. About 20 minutes before we landed, I shat myself. Bowel and bladder control in my newly damaged body were as hard to manage as the paralysis. It was a nightmare, and I was such an emotional mess.

Again, he was patient but pushed me out of my comfort zone. He had me get on the moving sidewalk when we landed in Charlotte. Just as quickly as I got on it, I flipped over backward. I was riding on my back, flipped in my wheelchair, in my poopy pants, through the airport terminal. At that point, I thought, *Okay, if you can survive this trip, you can do anything.* I should have been mortified, but I kept

98

moving forward. There was no other choice. During his time staying with me, we were featured on the *Today Show* for our fairytale love story and the groundbreaking trial surgery.

After that, it was up to the Badlands in Indiana to test run the adaptive custom hand-controlled Polaris ACE I would be racing in the GNCC series. While still in the hospital, I received an unexpected Polaris sponsorship to race in the GNCC series and was told I would be the only paralyzed racer in the Ace class. After years of dreaming about it, I finally had a factory ride, as it's called in the racing world. Flying on that high, I contacted the Shoei helmet company to let them know that their helmet had saved my life. As we talked, I told them about my factory ride and, to my delight and surprise, Shoei generously decided to gift me a new helmet. Sponsorships and everything I had dreamed about were coming to me at a time when I least expected it.

GNCC racing has six classes or divisions: ATV, dirt bike, side-by-side UTV, single-seat UTV, micros, and electronic bikes. Riding for Polaris, I moved from the ATV class, where the four-wheeled vehicles left my new body vulnerable to injury, to the single-seat UTV class. My single-seat Polaris ACE was more car-like than the quads I was used to racing, with a roof, protective bars, thicker doors, a five-point harness, and wrapped in bright pink SSI decals. The side panels were doors rather than the traditional solid roll cage, so I could easily get in. Even though my Polaris was quite different from the open-air style I was used to, the racing rush was still the same.

Getting into the Polaris for my first GNCC race post-injury, I was THRILLED—finally, some sense of normalcy. I had no fear of crashing in a single seat. I just wanted to do something I loved. Decked in my pink Simpson fire suit, black vans, and my special Shoei helmet, I was ready to race.

Travel became a dominant theme in my life, and I was just getting started. Six months after the accident, Jessica and I flew to Phoenix, Arizona, where we rented a car and drove to Las Vegas for the Fourth of July weekend. After that, Patient One and I spent a month together back in his Phoenix apartment, just the two of us. During this time, I learned a lot from Patient One, someone with three months more paralysis experience than I had, about becoming independent. The biggest lesson I learned from him was that I would not become more independent unless I pushed myself. It wasn't going to happen without effort.

Patient One had a truck. Transferring into this vehicle was difficult for me. Transferring my body from surface to surface in general was hard, forget going from my chair to a high surface like the truck. About two weeks into the stay, on a hot Arizona July day, I fell out of the truck during a transfer. He couldn't help get me off the ground. We had to call his friend to help me back into my chair. In some ways, it was comical, although at the time I had a meltdown. During the weeks I stayed with him, we did therapy together on the ground, working on floor transfers and working out in the apartment pool, and we were intimate. Once, while we were intimate, I peed on him. He shrugged it off. "No big deal." I cannot get over his gentle kindness and patience during those times.

This was my first taste of getting super personal with another wheelchair user. I had made great friends in rehab, but being together 24/7 without medical staff support, six months after the accident, there were a lot of "first" experiences. I was lucky to have someone who had recently been in my shoes teach me. I could also see by how well he was doing that I would get better with time, conditioning, and practice. Time to let my spastic bladder and other ailments heal.

Patient One gave me a sense of nonjudgmental normal with my spinal cord injury. He made me feel not as frustrated at a body out of my control. He showed me it was possible to build independence through hard work and enjoy life with paralysis. Yet, largely because of how it started, our relationship was doomed to fail. We were so deeply ingrained in this clinical trial and over the hope that we would walk again.

Not long after I returned home, Patient One told me he needed to focus on income and other priorities. He had come to the realization that dating someone who was newly injured was too emotionally intense, and he had enough of his own emotions to sort through and figure out. It was devastating for me. I cried for a month over it. At the same time, I understood his needs and felt grateful for the independence he taught me.

Reflection

It wasn't lost on me that not everyone going through a spinal cord injury was lucky enough to find someone like Patient One to be their mentor and friend. Someone willing to spend a full month helping me learn how to live with my physical disabilities. Someone who truly knows because he lives it. Holding that experience close to my heart fueled my future mission through the Wheel With Me Foundation. A foundation to provide people with the skills they need to live independent lives despite paralysis. I will always be grateful for the independent capabilities of a paraplegic Patient One demonstrated. He gave me hope and inspired me to pass that same hope on to others. If you asked me what personality trait is most important for someone going through the early stages of a devastating spinal cord injury, or any life-changing event, I would say the ability not to let fear of temporary embarrassment stop you.

13

Home

*"Fear not, for I am with you; be not dismayed, for I am
your God. I will strengthen you, yes, I will help you, I
will uphold you with My righteous right hand."*
—Isaiah 41:10 New King James Version

Finally, after a whirlwind of travel, it was time to go home and
stay home for a bit. Eighteen months before the accident, my parents
bought a home with an accessible basement in rural Iron Station,
North Carolina. Iron Station is about 40 minutes from the larger city
of Charlotte, North Carolina. A third extraordinary "coincidence"
when you count getting my supportive companion dog Roxanne
as the first and my entire Ohio family visiting us a few short weeks
before the accident as the second. *Yes,* I thought. One event could be
a random coincidence, but three? This was my destiny. *God had this
planned out for me a long time ago.*

My basement apartment was ready to go with everything I
needed to live adaptively: roll-in shower, grab bars beside the toilet, and wide doorways perfect for a wheelchair. We only had to put
higher toilets, a ramp, and an outdoor lift. When the lift was being
installed, the installer said, "I remember being here while this house
was under construction. We gave a quote for a lift before the home
was finished being built." Pre-injury, I didn't think much about the
accessibility of the basement except to joke about the shower. My
friends and I called our gigantic open shower a "porno shower"
because it was so big. *Who knew there were people in the world who
needed it?*

At the time, the typical waitlist for low-income accessible apartments in the Charlotte, North Carolina, area was two years. A two-
year wait if you could wait it out and get a coveted spot. At the

rehabilitation center, I met and made friends with other individuals whose only discharge living option was a nursing home. I felt incredibly fortunate.

Growing up, I had never met anyone using a wheelchair. In racing, you would hear of people getting injured, but usually, it was doing motocross, where riders sent their ATV or dirt bike airborne after hitting a jump. Due to my limited knowledge, I had a big learning curve when it came to understanding my disability and the importance of accessibility. You always hear of it and occasionally meet someone but never think of it or even let your mind consider that it could happen to you. The unthinkable happened to me. Not racing off-road as you might have predicted but as a motorcycle passenger.

Racing ATVs in the woods, dirt bike riding, and driving cars and motorcycles at high speeds were all risky endeavors requiring me to face fear. Yet, this was the scariest time of my life.

Financially, my parents made sure everything was set up for me before I got home. My Social Security Disability Insurance, Medicaid, lift arrangements, driving arrangements, and a million medical appointments. My parents hooked it up. I couldn't have gotten through those early days as fluidly as I did if I didn't have them. They helped me sort through a lot of the disability stuff. They were awesome advocates. Their emotional strength and practical help with finances supported me as I drifted through the shock.

Emotionally, I craved normalcy and routine. My former employers at the pediatric orthodontic office gave me this. While I was in the hospital, they found hand-controlled equipment that would allow me to clean teeth without using my legs. Then they invited me back to work. I could only manage two to three hours a day because I didn't quite have my bowel or bladder routines figured out and couldn't yet sit for long periods of time. Still, I was determined and drove myself to work using adaptive hand controls.

My young patients had the best reactions to me and my wheelchair. They were direct, often asking, "What's wrong with your legs?" in the most innocent way. I explained that a spine is like a railroad track. And that the message from our brain to our lower extremities is the train on that track. My railroad track was broken, I told them, so the message couldn't get through and my legs couldn't work. The children looked a little shocked at this before shaking their heads up and down and returning their attention to the teeth cleaning at hand. Returning to my job immediately for a few hours a week helped me feel normal in those early days.

Ultimately, my newly paralyzed body didn't cooperate. I had overestimated what I could physically do. I was only able to keep working part-time for four months. In those early days, working played a massive role in my disability adjustment and overall success, but, ultimately, working was physically too difficult to maintain. I wasn't quite ready to face my reality, and work made it all a little too real.

Back in my parents' home six months post-injury and unemployed, life quieted. For starters, family and friends had returned to their usual routines, so there were longer stretches when I was alone. Romantically, I was unattached. I self-isolated a lot at home largely out of necessity because daily tasks of living like dressing, moving around, and going to the bathroom took a lot of energy. Even though my physical wounds were healing, adjusting to living with the effects of a spinal cord injury takes time. I had to build up my chair-durance (as I call it). I hadn't heard about this in rehab, but it's very real. The body has to get used to seated life and build endurance for it not unlike building up endurance for any physical feat like long-distance running. It takes practice.

When night rolled around, I'd be ready for a distraction and to be social. I drank alcohol every day. I did have friends willing to carry me into their houses or anyplace else we went, so I didn't have to worry about finding accessible spaces. I did have to worry about my very spastic bladder, something else you must learn to manage with a spinal cord injury. This amounted to lots of time in the bathroom and accidents and chronic urinary tract infections. I just couldn't find that sweet spot of a reliable toileting routine. Taking an antibiotic while pouring alcohol down my throat was a double dose of trouble for my gut, leaving me feeling queasy. Those issues made going out less appealing.

On top of toileting and chair-durance work, I noticed I was losing several hours every day to such mundane tasks as dressing and showering and transferring from bed to wheelchair or wheelchair to car. I also spent time waiting on the floor for several hours each time I fell until someone came home to get me up. I fell because I wasn't strong enough to hold my body up with just my arms in order to move out of the wheelchair and swing myself to wherever I needed to go: bed, chair, toilet, car, etc. Imagine yourself trying to transfer with literal dead weight in the lower two-thirds of your body and you'll get the idea.

Despite obstacles, my social nature meant I was still game to try. If you have ever been injured or disabled, you know the feeling of vulnerability when you need help and grace. I so appreciate my friends and family for not making me feel weird about my new normal. Yet, not everyone shared that cool factor with my spastic bladder. Once, my childhood friend and I were riding somewhere in my car a couple of years after the accident. I told her that my then boyfriend and I recently had sex in the passenger seat. Without giving it much thought I added, "Of course, I peed a little bit. Just a couple of drops. It was an accident. I can't help it." When we arrived at our destination, my friend flung the car door open and leaped out, exclaiming, "Oh my gosh, I don't want to smell like pee." Her words hit me like a slap in the face.

Not too long after, I was at a wedding sharing a hotel room with a few of my closest childhood friends, and one of them commented, "Jesi, can you remove your medical supplies from the bathroom trash when you use it? I don't want to have to smell it." Her underlying tone was disgust. Disgust with my disability and all it entailed. I kindly replied, "You can handle it yourself if you are that concerned." I will not be made to feel bad about things out of my control.

While I was never shy about defending myself, the stress and complexities of socializing got the best of me. I began to retreat, spending more time at home where I felt emotionally safest. At home, I wore dresses, which made managing catheterizing myself easier. Another big way I coped was through online connections. I met another T4 paraplegic on Instagram. Someone injured longer than I had been and more experienced. Once we connected, I suddenly had someone to call if I fell on the floor. A routine started. I'd fall, and we'd spend an hour on FaceTime just trying to get me off the ground. I was never successful. I'd reach exhaustion and give up, but instead of pure frustration, we'd spend time laughing and joking a bit. Making those online connections, including joining spinal cord injury support groups early on, was one of my best decisions. Even so, sometimes it wasn't enough, and I still felt hopeless and alone. My big smiles and cheery thoughts posted online were as much a lame effort to convince myself and everyone else I was okay.

Settled into the basement, I found myself utterly alone with my thoughts. I was forced to confront what I'd lost. Taking inventory, the list was long, starting with my ability to walk. Next came bowel and bladder control, followed by no longer being able to manage my emotions in a "stable" manner, thanks to the traumatic brain injury. I had no filter. Whatever I was feeling came shooting out of my mouth. Of course, plagued as I was with nerve pain and spasms, I couldn't forget losing my pain-free existence. Then, between the pain, I needed to carve out three to four extra hours each day to manage simple tasks like getting changed and showered. And if I fell when I was alone, I might spend up to four hours scooting around and attempting to get back into my chair before help arrived. Endless doctor and therapy appointments ate up more time.

Adding to the misery, I was not the only one who had lost something. My parents grieved, too. Sometimes, when I was struggling to do something like get up off the floor after falling, my mom would walk into the kitchen and have a good cry. It went against her nature not to help her baby, but she knew I needed to struggle to find independence on the other side.

Sitting in my wheelchair in that basement apartment one day, I stared for hours at my .22 rifle, a Christmas gift from the previous year. I stared at it while thinking of myself as a cripple in a wheelchair. Hopeless and helpless. I also did this every time I fell out of my wheelchair and onto the floor, but at that moment I felt this label of "cripple" more than ever. Adding to this pitiful picture, I thought about how there was a flood of friends and family initially supporting and rallying around after the accident. But it had been three months. Long enough for the fanfare to wane. People had to get on with their lives, and I couldn't blame them. My sorry self was old news. They had their own problems and struggles. Mine was mine and mine alone to deal with; no one was going to save me. My princess crown crashed to the floor. Shattered. Never to be replaced. Sulking in the stink of my existence, every rifle suicide scenario went through my mind.

13. Home

I held the small silver bullet in my hand, wondering if it would be enough. Tears filled my eyes as I thought of the physical and emotional pain I was experiencing. Then, even more tears followed as I thought of the pain my family had just endured in my recent near-death experience and the additional pain my death would cause. I told myself to make a choice. Do it for me or don't do it for my family. Several hours went by as I grappled with the decision.

I wish I could wrap this dilemma up in a neat little package and serve it to you. The truth is that protecting family and friends was a factor but not the only factor pulling me towards life. Another was being unconvinced a .22 rifle used for hunting small animals and training new shooters was capable of doing the job. It wasn't very powerful, so I knew it might worsen matters. Grandma sent me back for a reason: Who was I to go against my newfound God's will? I finally grabbed the gun, went upstairs, and asked my dad to lock it up in his safe. Little did my parents know the battle with life I had just won.

Little by little, what felt like total darkness at first became easier and more hopeful. It started about a year after the accident. First, I began a praying routine. Leaning into faith gave me strength and a more optimistic mindset. I accepted that, moment to moment, I had only two very different choices, to focus on everything I lost or to focus on what I still had and still was. I'm not going to lie. I focused a lot in those early days on what I had lost. But at the same time, I fought hard to keep reminding myself of the good things: a roof over my head, a loving family, and my dog Roxanne. Taking things one day at a time, I aimed to maintain a calm, level head. Whenever I did that, I felt successful. This positivity and faith carried me through the next big challenge: accepting that I was not one of the successful participants in the clinical trial.

I had several follow-up appointments with clinical trial staff after the implant surgery. The first was 30 days out, then three months, six months, one year, and two years. During the appointments, my American Spinal Injury Association (ASIA) exam was done to determine if there had been any progress since the surgery. Each time, it was a disappointment; there were no changes. I remained a Grade A on the ASIA scale, meaning I had a complete lack of motor and sensory function below the point of injury. The scale includes grades A, B, C, D, and E, with E meaning all neurologic function is intact. By the two-year marker, the in-person part of this experiment ended. While they continued to see me once a year to check if I was still alive, my official ranking stated "no change."

Of the 19 total participants in the first clinical trial, three people died for reasons unrelated to the trial. Seven of the remaining 16 of us (43.8 percent) improved neurological functioning to various degrees, with a few subjects moving from complete to incomplete spinal cord injuries, regaining some physical movement below the origin of their spinal cord injury. While eight patients showed deterioration, I was among the group of three who showed no change (https://www.invivotherapeutics.com/).

I was not going to walk unassisted any time soon. God was working miracles in my life, but fixing my spinal cord wasn't going to be one of them. This reckoning with the truth came to me in waves since denial ran deep. Denial cemented in with months of private and public declarations of my intention to beat my spinal cord injury and walk again one day. Admitting I wouldn't walk again felt like quitting on my goals. I didn't want to lose or give up on this long-standing dream, but the evidence was clear and undeniable.

For the first time since this whirlwind of an injury, I compromised. I would see what this wheel life offered me versus making walking my priority. I still hoped to walk again and planned on working towards getting better, potentially walking again, but I also wanted to embrace my life in the here and now with what I could currently do.

Accepting that the clinical trial wouldn't save me, I considered ways to save myself. Most of my day was spent navigating being newly injured, with ongoing difficulty managing my spastic bladder, at the same time pushing through chronic urinary tract infections and those annoying and sometimes painful muscular spasms. Also, headaches, moodiness, and brain fog, thanks to the traumatic brain injury. Despite my social fears and physical challenges, I'd had enough of sitting at home. I can't say for sure what the defining moment was, but at some point, I figured I was going to feel crappy no matter what, so I might as well push past my fears and do something fun. Join the party. After all, I was single and ready to mingle.

14

Community Is Everything

"Jesi Stracham, Ms. Wheelchair North Carolina USA, lives in Iron Station, North Carolina, and went to Central Piedmont Community College. She is a racer in the GNCC Series and races for Racer Tech Polaris Factory Racing in a specialized hand controlled machine and was featured on the Today Show *covering the clinical trial she was involved in for her spinal surgery. Jesi is a T4 complete paraplegic caused by a 2015 motorcycle accident and has 19 screws and 2 rods fusing her spine. She is a volunteer and mentor at the Rehab Facility with the SCI Life Group. Stracham's platform, 'Wheel with Me: Using Obstacles to Live Life to the Fullest,' is to inspire people to live life to its fullest potential no matter what obstacles arise in life."*
—Ms. Wheelchair USA
social media post, July 24, 2016

Deciding to be more social and active, I did the same thing I had done with racing. I threw myself into it. I started by taking a solo cross-country trip with my Volkswagen Jetta to visit wheelchair users I met through social media. A trip made possible only because my wheel friends had accessible places to stay. Networking in this way did a lot to lift my spirits and build an all-important wheel community. Yet, it did nothing to stop my unhealthy, destructive behaviors. I was no longer smoking but continued to drink alcohol daily, indulge in junk food, and, for reasons I still can't fully explain, return to the rush of stimulants. Anything to get through the day.

The therapist I swam with at rehab told me about an adaptive adventure event at the Whitewater Center. It was a day of fun where teams of five, including regular ability and disabled participants, whitewater raft, kayak, paddleboard, zip-line, and navigate ropes courses.

While doing the Whitewater Center activities, I met this ginger crip named Kevin. He was one of my first wheel friends, and we had a good time together. Kevin was a tough-love kind of guy. He called me out on my shit. A friend to help me stay positive and build grit. Seven years later, I was in Kevin's wedding party. One of the best friendships blossomed from that early adventure event, showing me my first glimpse of the power of community.

While building my wheel community, I started spending more time with family and my most supportive friends. Johnathan, now my sister Jodi's fiancé, is a prime example. Johnathan was a kindred spirit, as we were born on the same day. Any idea I had to push my limits, Johnathan was there to make it happen. For example, one day Johnathan took me to a foam pit at an action sports complex and carried me up the stairs so I could attempt to flip my wheelchair. I failed, but we had a damn good time.

Another guy friend I hung out with I had met through mutual friends right after I was paralyzed. We had some things in common and got pretty close. Taco was a dirt bike racer. He knew I needed a diversion to get out of the house, so he invited me to travel with him while he raced. Taco's dad joked I was his informal team manager as we traveled together to many of his dirt bike racing events in those early post-injury years. Taco was an amazing friend and showed me how it's possible to be platonic friends with a guy without ever crossing a line. He accepted me the way I was and even installed my portable hand controls into his van so I could help drive to the races.

On social media, I learned of an opportunity to be involved in the Ms. Wheelchair USA competition. Ms. Wheelchair USA is a smaller-scale version of Ms. Wheelchair America. It's a fundraising event organized by the Dane Foundation, a nonprofit organization founded in memory of Dane Edward Moser and based in Ohio. Its mission is to provide clothing, toiletries, household cleaning supplies, and other necessities for people with disabilities.

I noticed the event was going to be held near my hometown of Canton, Ohio, so I could use it as an excuse to visit family at the same time I participated. I applied and was accepted to represent North Carolina or, more accurately, the Carolinas, since we were a smallish group of about 20 female participants. To pay for it, I fundraised. Fundraising kept me busy until the event, which was held in the Akron High School gym, the gym that professional basketball superstar LeBron James remodeled.

As a LeBron James fan, I was excited to see the gym because of all the things he'd done for northeastern Ohio, specifically the city of Cleveland. It didn't disappoint. The souped-up LeBron James Arena shined in a typically drab, well-worn high school. Spaulding supplied a new gym floor, bleacher seats for 1,800, six NCAA models, and hydraulic baskets. New lighting that is eight times brighter than what had been in place. Renovated locker rooms for both the boys and girls teams. Renovated offices for the boys and girls coaching staff. A new athletic training treatment room. A new sound system. A "dedication wall" impressively chronicling in pictures James's time at St. Vincent-St. Mary and his four close friends who completed the Fab Five—Dru Joyce III, Romeo Travis, Willie McGee, and Sian Cotton.

Sadly, we competed in the auditorium, not the gym, but seeing it was still fun. Racing in the GNCC series and having some practice doing media interviews about the clinical trials and my paralysis gave me enough confidence to hold my own in the judging categories: how well we presented our platform, the topic of the platform itself, poise, and formal wear. Although I never advanced to be crowned Ms. Wheelchair USA, I did receive second runner-up. More satisfying than that, I met many amazing women doing incredible things out in the world. I also wore a pretty dress, posed, and smiled wide

Second Runner-Up in Ms. Wheelchair USA pageant.

for the camera. It made me feel sexy and like a girl again. It also helped solidify my platform or life ambition to use obstacles to live life fully.

It all appeared to be tidy. Yet, the mess was covered with a big smile and nice clothes. I wasn't really "living life to the fullest"; that was more of my dream than day-to-day reality. Inside, way deep down, lived a scared kid drowning in a badly damaged body, trying desperately to stay engaged in life. Being busy felt like coming up for air to breathe.

In spite of my fears and doubts, I pushed on. And it paid off. Making wheel friends was a massive turning point in adjusting to my injury. I went from shock, depression, and hopelessness to a place of social acceptance. Being around a community of individuals who had embraced the wheel life allowed me to accept myself as a disabled person while learning how to adapt at the same time. It helped ease the transition to my new goal to stop focusing so much on walking and begin to focus on what the wheel life had to offer.

I begin participating in every adaptive sport I could, the more extreme, the better, like wheelchair motocross (WCMX). WCMX, where you take your wheelchair to the skate park, became my new obsession. It looked so cool watching others do it on television. I decided to give it a try. My friend Johnathan was always down to try those types of adventures. There was no better feeling than launching the chair down a ramp at a park. It wasn't pretty watching me as a skateboard competitor. I was more of a face plant professional than anything else, but I had fun, which was the point. I also tried adaptive sports like water-skiing, snow skiing, hand cycling, and curling.

Curling especially was incredible for social fun, but it was also a chance to mingle with the public after our sessions on the ice, with mixed results. O was my curling bestie and an immigrant from Mongolia. A paraplegic like me, O was both a mother and a dedicated, talented curler on track to become a Paralympian. One day, after practice at my home club, we drove to downtown Charlotte to satisfy our craving for ramen noodles. Driving my Volkswagen Passat, I parked in an accessible parking space. The access row, an extra lane essential for us to maneuver in and out of the car, was on the passenger side.

After lunch, O and I returned to the car. Just as we were starting

With my best friend in crime, Johnathan.

the long process of getting in, folding up our wheelchairs, and transferring into the car, another car approached. Instead of choosing a regular parking space, they parked on our access lane.

We approached. "Hey, you have just parked in an access lane for wheelchair users. Will you please park elsewhere so we can get in the car?"

The man replied, "Well, there's nowhere else to park."

Not one to hold back my opinions, I told him: "For your convenience, you take away our independence? That's not right!"

The driver didn't like being schooled by me. He stepped out of the car, approaching us while his female passenger yelled insults, accusing us of being selfish and inconsiderate.

Again, not one to hold back, I let insult lady have it: "Hey, I'm just trying to help you avoid a $500 fine. You don't have to be such a cunt!"

Everyone fumed. Then—oh man—it was on.

The driver screamed, "You called my fiancée a cunt!"

I yelled back, "That's what she's acting like."

The man's voice lowered, taking on a condescending tone. "Just sit in your wheelchair."

Sarcastically, I replied: "Oo, burn."

His companion continued to cuss as he got back in the car. Then she screamed, "Hurry up and take your fucking wheelchair apart!"

Not backing down, I replied, "You better hope nothing like this ever happens to you that you're in this situation dealing with assholes like yourself."

Spit flying from his mouth, he hissed back, "Wow, I've never heard anyone play the victim card so badly. Do you always play the victim?"

Getting the last word before they drove off, I said, "Disability doesn't discriminate. I'm just being real."

After the parking lot incident, I decided it was time to use my social media platform to share my experiences as a way to show the public that I was still a person despite having a physical disability. You do not need to treat people with disabilities with less integrity than anyone else you pass on the street. What happened to me could happen to you. We are not so different. Empathy and compassion help all of us be better humans.

Reflection

It turns out that community is everything. We need each other to support our ability to achieve success. To be in our bubble, to see each other's struggles, and to cheer each other on. We must fight back against our self-sabotaging tendencies of being alone and isolated. To prevent our attempts to insulate ourselves from each other. Being brave doesn't mean you are not afraid. It means you ARE afraid but choose to put yourself out there anyway. As for the parking lot incident, over time I've come to realize that getting worked up and angry only hurts me. These days I have more emotional control using words to diffuse rather than escalate situations.

15

Frustration of Paralysis

*"For I consider that the sufferings of this present time
are not worthy to be compared with the glory which
shall be revealed in us."*
—Romans 8:18 New King James Version

By year two of paralysis, everyone thought my activity level was that of an athlete, someone fit and disciplined. After all, I was second runner-up in Ms. Wheelchair USA, participating in adaptive sports like WCMX and curling, racing the GNCC circuit with a Polaris factory ride, looking equally sporty on the dirt bike circuit to cheer Taco on. Each event documented through social media posts, I looked like the picture of health.

Still, even though I looked healthy, I was anything but. My social life had improved considerably, but whenever I was home, I slept all day. In the evening, I smoked cannabis to prepare for the Netflix binge sessions that lasted well into the night. I ate what I wanted when I wanted. Once, I ate over half a jar of peanut butter in one sitting. I threw up shortly after I put the lid on the jar. *Whoops.* Other times I treated myself with cheesecake. I bought the small frozen cheesecakes from the grocery store thinking each was one serving rather than enough calories for one person for a whole day. I kept up my habit of drinking alcohol daily, even though it screwed up my already fragile bowel routine. Exercise wasn't a priority either, even though being in the wheelchair meant I was burning fewer calories than ever. Like so many who become paralyzed, I was steadily gaining weight. Thirty pounds in the first two years post-accident.

If it weren't for how much I was enjoying my newfound wheel community and staying busy hanging out with Jessica, Johnathan, or Taco at dirt bike races, I might have cocooned up at home forever.

Yet, that wasn't the way it went down. Instead, I signed up to attend an all-female adaptive curling camp. I wanted to get better. Better not only at curling but at life. In addition to curling, I was starting to follow and listen to motivational speakers like Eric Thomas (*Beast Mode*), Lisa Nichols (*Step Into Your Purpose*) and Inky Johnson (*Pain Is Our Teacher*). Each message fed me with positive messaging from brilliant minds and through personal journaling.

The curling camp was in Cape Cod, Massachusetts, and I was staying in the hotel room alone. When I checked into the hotel, the front desk staffer handed me the key to my accessible room. The room had two queen-sized beds. I picked one of them to sleep in and laid out my clothes on the other one. I hadn't been in the room for very long when I fell trying to transfer myself from the wheelchair to the bed. *Boom.* I hit the floor hard right in between the two beds. My phone was with me. I thought, *Great, I can videotape this for my online paralysis support group.* We had been supporting one another in learning how to do transfers.

Video camera in place on the dresser in front of me, I took a few deep breaths and rested for a few minutes. Moving my legs with my hands into the best position, I tried to use my arm strength to get back on my chair. Once again, I fell on the floor. It was not going well for me that day. I was frustrated and in a weak moment, very focused on my struggle. On a whim, I recorded myself venting about my paraplegia. Calling it "Frustration of Paralysis," I later posted the video to YouTube.

Here's the full video transcript. Warning: there will be swear words. You can also watch the original video on YouTube.

Frustration of Paralysis

Note: This is MY personal experience living with a spinal cord injury. The views and language expressed in this video solely reflect my own and are not related to my affiliates in any way, shape, or form. I wanted to share the ugly truth of a rough day in my life.

Please keep negativity to yourselves.

**Update: I still have days like this from time to time.

Thank you for watching.

15. Frustration of Paralysis

So, I'm going to get straight to the point. If you are sensitive—a millennial or whatever—if you can't handle cussing, if you can't handle the truth, if you can't handle the realization of life, I'm going to need you to just go ahead and exit out of this video. Now.

Moving forward... To all of you ignorant people that think paralysis is just being in a wheelchair, you're sadly mistaken.

Most of us can't take a shit on our own. We can't piss on our own. We have to shove a catheter, which if you don't know what a catheter is, it's a small tube that we shove up our urethra. If you've been to the hospital, you've probably had one. Yeah, we have to do that every time we pee. Oh, God. Who knew?! Most of us are on what's called a bowel program. This is where to poop we have to either stick a finger up our butt, take a suppository, enemas, or some other type of object up our ass. Sounds like a good time, doesn't it? We're having real fun.

Oh! Do you see that wheelchair? I fell out of it. Now I'm on the floor. I should just get back up and get back in it. Right? Why am I being lazy? Why am I sitting on the floor? None of you understand what it takes to get back in that fucking chair. None of you understand what it takes to travel. All of the medical fucking bullshit that I have to pack in my suitcase. Every fucking time I wanna fucking go somewhere. Or the fact that if I go out of state my in-state Medicaid, because it's North Carolina, doesn't cover my medical bills if something happens to me in another state. Did you know that?

These are the realizations of having a disability that mainstream media doesn't let you see. It's not easy. It's not an easy fight, and I'm sick of able-bodied people thinking that we are just lazy, because we are not. Nine times out of 10, we live our life 100 times more than you will ever think of living yours.

The whole purpose of this video initially was to show a floor transfer for a wheelchair support group that I'm in just to show them how I get back in my chair when I'm alone. Traveling. Living my life. Mind you, it's February 21, 2017. I lost the use of my legs on January 18, 2015. I'm a little over two years and I'm traveling alone because I am a person too. Just because I am in a wheelchair doesn't mean I can't live my life. So stop treating us like we are some caged animal. Or a child that can't take care of themselves. Stop trying to help us unless we ask you for help.

It's unbelievable, but, yeah ... the next time you think "They are just in a chair," how about you think again? Because to get back in this chair, I've got to move mattresses. You see, I still can't floor transfer strongly. There's a good chance the first time I'm not going to make it. If I do, then hell yeah, more power to me. But, in all reality, the chances of that are pretty dang slim. I'm not going to lie. [I moan and groan attempting to get in the chair, then fall back down to the floor.]

See, told you I wouldn't make it. Do you want to know why? Because my legs don't work and half my core doesn't work. My injury level is right here under my chest [I point just below my breasts]. Do you see that? That's a T5 injury. So somebody that's a paraplegic, which is what I am considered, doesn't mean I can do what another paraplegic can do with a T12 injury that's down here [I point below the belly button].

We can't do the same things. So stop being like "Oh this person in a wheelchair can do it. Why can't you?" or "Oh, I know this person in a wheelchair. Do you know them too?" We don't all know each other! Just because you are walking, do you know that other walker over there? ...Or just because you are Asian, do you know that other Asian over there? No. Stop categorizing us.

[I make a second attempt to transfer floor to chair and fail.] See. Two tries now. Still didn't work, did it? So we'll take a fucking different approach. How about that? [I cry.] I'm so frustrated. I get frustrated and then I cry because this is my life. This is my daily life. I don't get to wake up and just put my pants on. Go to the toilet. Get to pee. Like you. Then get to stand in the mirror, brush my teeth, and do my hair and makeup. I don't have that. I don't have that freedom that you do.

So the next time that you catch your child, cousins, parents, friends, strangers, or anyone staring at somebody in a wheelchair you need to tell them to think about that. Because we go through enough. We don't need your judgment as well.

Eventually, I got myself up off the floor. My resentment and anger came with me too. Two years post-accident, I lived in a state of being perpetually pissed off. Despite anything optimistic I would post or talk about, the internal lens viewing myself and my circumstances was dark. I was the victim. *Life is cruel and unfair to me as a physically disabled woman.*

When traveling, I'd seek evidence of inaccessibility to feed my negative emotions. Of course, that was never hard to find. Sidewalks ending in steps, restaurants I couldn't get into, non-disabled people using the only disabled toilet stall when I had to go. The struggle to find accessible parking. Inner peace was elusive. I became the struggle, and being the struggle left me miserable much of the time.

When I flew home to Charlotte shortly after recording "Frustration of Paralysis," my longtime mentor and sponsor for the Ms. Wheelchair America competition picked me up from the airport. As she took me home, she told me about a new adaptive CrossFit program, Project Momentum Fitness. The founder of Project Momentum has cerebral palsy, so she is another person with a disability who is teaching fitness. It just made sense, and I was excited about participating.

Adaptive CrossFit got me going on serious weight training. I hadn't picked up weights since before I was paralyzed. I didn't even know I could work out from my wheelchair. I was excited to get started. I partnered with a coach. She was great and taught me so much about adaptive CrossFit. When the Project Momentum grant money ran out, the founder herself took over, training everyone. Having such as skilled and passionate trainer was one of my biggest inspirations for becoming a fitness coach. The huge impact she has on all of her athletes is something to admire and try to emulate. I remember the day, after weeks of consistent strength training, when I threw my suitcase into the trunk of my car by myself for the first time. I thought, *Hell yeah, this is why I lift weights!* I owe that to my CrossFit coaches.

I quit drinking alcohol around the time I started my personal development journey. I started having bowel accidents after every night I drank, and it was just too much to deal with and incompatible with my fitness goals. Topping it off, one crazy night of drinking happened where I found myself following my drunk companions onto the freeway. I was alone in my car, buzzed, and noticed we were all going the wrong way. Even a third unrelated car followed us the wrong way. Fortunately, we all were able to get turned around. This scary and potentially deadly experience rattled me. I decided to quit. Even trying to have a drink here or there, the same thing would happen with my bowels. It simply wasn't worth it.

After I posted "Frustration of Paralysis," I noticed it was getting a lot of views. I always knew I was the type of person never to hold back raw emotion, but until "Frustration of Paralysis" was released, it hadn't occurred to me that my skill of speaking impromptu, openly, and freely might generate public interest. Speaking within my tight circle, we agreed I should keep going and try intentionally to build a public platform.

Of course, committing to grow my social media platform by educating, motivating, and helping others wasn't entirely altruistic. I needed to eat. Yes, I had disability checks and lived with my parents, paying a modest rent. I also budgeted myself to the penny. Still, I lived in poverty. If I wanted to pull out of poverty enough to have any hope of buying a home or going on holidays, finding other income streams wasn't optional. It was essential. I secured a few brand sponsorships with products I already used and partnerships as my social media platform grew.

Regardless of how much cash I could make, I refused to promote anything I didn't actually use. I was done with the lying and cheating of my youth since nothing good ever came from it. The habit of lying conflicted with the person I had become once I was thrown off that supercharged motorcycle. Above everything else, I wanted to be honest. A person of integrity. Product promotions that were true and real, though, seemed like a no-brainer and are something I continue to do today.

The second reason I wanted to grow a platform was to spread the word about a nonprofit I founded called Wheel With Me Foundation. Still racing for Polaris, I became sponsored by a clothing company called Justified Cultures in Yuma, Arizona. They mostly sponsor supercross racers but agreed to sponsor me for my GNCC races. The owner offered to create a T-shirt to donate a portion of the profits to a charity of my choice. Searching, I couldn't find one that supported the independence of wheelchair users in the manner I wished. That was, and always will be, my passion. When I told the owner about the need for the newly injured to have bridge support to build independence after rehabilitation stays, she generously suggested we start a nonprofit and even offered to fill out the filing paperwork, provide start-up funding, and manage it. I readily agreed. Yet another gift from God (and the owner of Justified Cultures) that fell into my lap.

Inspiration for the name Wheel With Me came from my friend

Taco, the guy who let me tag along with him to his dirt bike races. Taco would say, "Ride with me," which means hang with me. I'd respond, "No man, it's wheel with me." We'd laugh, and from then on, we'd say, "Wheel with me!" and the name stuck, just like our friendship.

When the time came to name the new nonprofit, I thought of Taco and all of the wheel friends I'd made since my spinal cord injury. I'd learned how the simple yet profound act of inviting others to join in just as they are can change lives. Confidently, I said, "Wheel With Me," and the Wheel With Me Foundation was born. For three years, until her well-deserved retirement to spend more time with her family, the owner of Justified Cultures stayed on with Wheel With Me voluntarily as we worked together, arranging educational and community-building opportunities for wheelchair users aimed at empowerment and independence.

Taco, who has a natural gift of knowing many people and being generous with introductions, introduced me to Jamie and her husband, Jimmy, who were new to Charlotte. I liked both of them immediately, but I was especially stoked after meeting Jamie, a potential new female friend with similar interests. I spent so much time with guys I felt the need for more female friends. The day after Taco made the introduction, I slid into her Instagram direct messages saying, "Hey, Girl! I know you are new to the area and could use some friends here, and I'm looking to make female friends! Let's hang out!" She was receptive. We made a doggy play date for Roxanne and their dog, Marley, at the local dog bar. Jamie and I continued to hit it off. We talked, and I learned she is a powerful, badass girl boss. A Canadian immigrant, she had learned how to do touch-up paint on cars and was building her own company in the States. On top of that, she managed Jimmy's race schedule, their house, his merch line, and her health and fitness.

Jamie gave me my first glimpse of what it means to be a powerhouse of a woman. Not just because of her accomplishments but because of her character. One time, we were taking a walk with the dogs. I started telling her a story about another woman, painting her in a negative light. Jamie stopped me. "Jesi, I don't do that." Feeling a bit embarrassed, I gave a one-word reply. "What?" Jamie elaborated: "I don't talk about other people negatively. It doesn't make me

The woman who helped me find my inner badass, Jamie (left).

feel good, and it's not a nice thing to do." Jamie's moral strength and wisdom in that moment impressed me. As our friendship deepened, there were many more moments like this one, ultimately inspiring me to be a better person.

16

Tough Mudder

*"I'm laughing. I posted on my IG story this morning. I
had three people ask me what I was doing up at 4 AM.
Some people think I'm nuts. No alarm clock is needed.
I'm driven. Focused. I have a purpose."*
—journal entry during Tough Mudder years

Around the same time I started CrossFit, I had a disabled friend
who was signed up for the Charlotte Spartan Race. Something happened, and she couldn't do it. "Jesi, would you like to take my place as
an adaptive athlete? I promise you, you'll have a blast." She explained
that while the event was primarily for non-disabled athletes, as an
adaptive athlete I would be financially and team-supported by an
organization called More Hearts Than Scars. Impulsive as always, I
thought about it for about 10 seconds before deciding it would be a
cool opportunity for me to try something new. "Sure, I'm game to try
it."

I woke up before the sun on a Saturday to drive to my first Spartan Race. It was a bit of a dilemma what to wear, considering my toileting issues. Since we were going to be wet and rolling around in the
mud for hours, I decided to forgo catheters and let my bladder spasm,
essentially peeing myself out on course. Using a foley (an indwell-
ing catheter you don't need to insert each time you empty your bladder manually) never crossed my mind. I settled on a simple wardrobe
of leggings, compression socks, a compression top, and old tennis
shoes. Once there, I quickly met my adaptive athlete support team,
and, almost immediately, it was go time.

As I wheeled to the starting line, my heart was pounding. I had
no idea what to expect; it was cold and rainy, so I was prepared to be
cold and wet. The countdown started, and we were off through the

starting corral. Of course, in the chair I was slower than the runners, especially because I hadn't physically trained. As runners whizzed past me, most were kind and supportive. Still, because it was a timed competition, some were rude and even made negative comments because my wheelchair sometimes inconvenienced them. Those comments weren't what I focused on, though. I kept my eyes looking forward and strove to do my best. Music was blasting, crowds were cheering, and I felt this huge high each time I conquered an obstacle.

Obstacles like the eight-foot box. This giant eight-foot-tall wooden box with a rope along the wall you used to climb over it. A booster was available for female competitors, but because I lack leg movement and most of my core, my More Hearts Than Scars volunteers were available for as-needed extra assistance on the wall. Once you scale the box, there are stairs on the way down in the back, so my team navigated with me doing as much as possible on my own. We did that again and again through 20 total obstacles.

There was laughter, tears, and sometimes near-complete exhaustion for me and my adaptive athlete volunteers. Crossing the finish line, I was covered head to toe in mud except for my white teeth, bared in a huge smile. It was a blast. The Spartan Race gave me that same adrenaline rush I felt and loved competing on my Polaris single seat, except I was more mentally challenged. I intuitively knew endurance events were a perfect motivator to keep working out and eating healthy, each effort boosting my confidence and self-esteem in every aspect of life.

Before fully catching my breath from finishing that first Spartan Race, I decided to commit to the Spartan Trifecta, meaning I'd have to finish the entire Spartan series: Sprint, Super, and Beast in the same season. That first race checked off the sprint. More Hearts Than Scars again stepped up to fund the longer Spartan Super race later in the year. At the Spartan Super, I reconnected with volunteer Sarah Fox, who stood out to me with her leadership skills and intuitive ability to assist me perfectly without helping too much or too little during my first time on the course.

In between the Spartan Sprint and Super, More Hearts Than Scars offered sponsorship for me to try a Tough Mudder Half. At the Tough Mudder Half, I met the team that would also be working on each obstacle with me. Tough Mudder did not disappoint—except when we finished the course and I wasn't ready to be done. I had SO MUCH FUN. Tough Mudder had the same adrenaline rush and physical challenge as Spartan Races, but the team aspect made it perfect for an adaptive athlete like me. We truly helped one another; sometimes I could help my teammates, too, which felt so good. We aimed to complete and keep going rather than racing against the clock or anyone else.

By the time we finished the Tough Mudder Half, it was evening. Many who had helped our endeavors were gearing up for a Toughest Mudder or overnight event. This piqued my interest. The distance was grueling. Several hours were spent pushing through the woods, wading through the mud, and climbing over and under man-made obstacles. You started and finished as a team. Athletes also had the option to skip any obstacle they didn't feel comfortable doing.

At one point, my volunteer Sarah from the Spartan Super and I talked. "Sarah, you have been doing Tough Mudders for years and love it. I did a half and am hooked. It makes a lot more sense for a wheelchair user like me, plus they have these cool overnight endurance event options I want to try. Would you consider being my person?" In an instant, Team Wheel With Me was born.

The next week, Sarah and I loaded up the car. That's how fast we put Team Wheel With Me together to do my first Toughest Mudder course. It was eight hours overnight doing laps on the course. Sarah and I and the rest of the Wheel With Me team found the atmosphere very supportive and fun! A nonprofit called Oscar Mike was awesome enough to loan us an offroad-style wheelchair for the course, making things easier for both me and the team. While Spartan obstacles are more military style, using natural elements, Tough Mudder incorporates a zany array of man-made construction obstacles. This gives it a fun, party atmosphere with everyone cheering for one another, regardless of ability.

Wheelchair athletes were very rare in Tough Mudder endurance events, but I could see the potential for adaptive athletes right away. Through doing more Tough Mudders, I made a friend and mentor in California native Tyson "Superman" Perry, who, like me, is a spinal cord injury survivor. Tyson holds the world record as the first person to complete a Tough Mudder event with his Team Go Hard. Sometimes, having another person who knows what it feels like mentor you makes all the difference. We quickly became each other's number one fan.

> After finishing Toughest Midwest, I tell Sarah, "I'm not sure how, but we are doing The World's Toughest Mudder, and I am getting the holy grail!" Somehow, we pulled this incredible team together! 9 mudders later, we're crazy enough to do it again! I plan to conquer 24 hours of the World's Toughest Mudder Course with a team of incredible individuals!
>
> —social media post

I had fun at endurance events, but, if I wanted to survive them, I had no choice but to dive into physical conditioning and a strong mindset. Between CrossFit, better nutrition, and training for Tough Mudders, I lost the 30 pounds of fat gained during my first year post-accident while adding muscle. Functional muscle that helped with my independence.

My adventures extended beyond the courses since travel was required to get to Tough Mudders. I drove to Las Vegas one year to participate in the World's Toughest Mudder. En route, I decided to stop off at one of my favorite travel destinations, Phoenix, Arizona, to meet up with a friend, an influencer under his Wheels2Walking platform. Besides catching up, we decided to create content at one of the most accessible gyms in the country, Ability 360.

Everything was going fine until I had to pee. Transferring to the toilet, I noticed a lot of blood. I had just finished my period, so this didn't make sense. I stuffed toilet paper in my pants to soak it up and went to hit my workout. We recorded some bomb content, finished our workout, and returned to his house. I transferred out of his car, and there was a wet spot on the seat. I thought it was pee; I kept apologizing for leaving a mark on his seat. My favorite thing about my wheel friends is their kindness when things like that happen. They don't mind helping to clean it up. Inside the house, I went straight to the bathroom to get a new pull-up on. There was blood everywhere. It wasn't pee. I came out of the bathroom. It was time for a candid talk.

"Bro, I know this is the last thing you want to do, but I need you to look at my vagina. I did something to it." Alternating between laughing hard and grave concern, we set up a mat. I did a floor transfer onto the mat, got on my back, and then put my legs up while he gloved up. Equipped with gauze and an ice pack, he examined me and solved the mystery. I had ripped the inside lip of my labia about an inch when I transferred to that toilet.

I probably should have gone into the emergency department immediately, but wheelchair users are a whole other level of toughness. Sometimes, it feels like every other day brings a new medical symptom or complication. After waiting it out overnight, the bleeding hadn't stopped. I had to go to the hospital. Upon arriving at the hospital, I asked the doctor, "How fast will this heal? I have to spend 24 hours in the mud in two weeks and can't have a fresh wound in a sensitive place." Two stitches on the inside crest of my labia, and I was good to go. As outrageous as this story is, events like it still happen to me. Lessons in humility, trust, and keeping a sense of humor along with good people around you.

The Wheel With Me team continued attending Tough Mudder events for four seasons. We rotated through volunteers each time, but Sarah remained our leader. I was not great at explaining the best ways I needed to be supported to complete each obstacle, but Sarah did an excellent job briefing everyone before the event. She communicated exactly what I needed and the safest way to do it. She even kept me on track. Having those Tough Mudder events marked on my calendar motivated me. Because I committed hard, I now have the privilege of being the only wheelchair user to complete the Tough Mudder Holy Grail three times. This endurance series includes Tough Mudder Infinity, Toughest Mudder, and World's Toughest Mudder. That's one daytime and two overnight events lasting between eight and 24 hours. Imagine headlamps bobbing in the woods. It is so cool.

As I write this, new adaptive athletes are wearing the special adaptive athletes course bibs. I am so proud to have served on the adaptive athlete board for Tough Mudder, paving the way for future adaptive athletes to participate in the now-established Tough Mudder Adaptive Athlete program. A program where athletes earn a special course bib, assistance securing team members, and opportunities for waived course fees. Although health issues required me to retire my bib after completing my last World's Toughest Mudder in 2022 in favor of less high-impact activities, the legacy lives on. It's difficult to put into words what we were able to accomplish on course.

My first World's Toughest Mudder with Sarah (right).

My last World's Toughest Mudder with Sarah (standing).

Reflection

I'm an extremist. When I commit to something, I commit hard. That personality trait got me in plenty of trouble in my earlier years, especially when it came to disobeying my parents, cheating in my relationships, and having a party lifestyle. It also has helped me maintain a wide circle of friends in my pursuit of fitness. That same commitment to the Wheel With Me team helped us complete 15 Tough Mudders, most of them overnight events. To pay for it, I raised money and sponsorships. I will be forever grateful to a lot of generous volunteers and supporters. Many endurance events and fitness centers, such as the YMCA, offer sliding scale fees, whether you're disabled or not. Abundant opportunity is one of the many reasons I love America and living in this country. Worldwide, web-based technology is full of free information on specific techniques to become more holistically fit. Initiative drove my early success, not financial resources.

17

Ice Queen

"A spinal cord injury robs you of more than meets the eye. In addition to the loss of lower extremity motor control, you often lose bowel and bladder control. Being a young woman this dealt a blow to my confidence. I often felt insecure that I would pee everywhere, and was often embarrassed if my friends saw my catheters or diapers. Something my weight loss journey has given me is confidence in being sexy even with the struggles my spinal cord injury brings. Thankfully my waist is small enough that I can fit in children's Pull-Ups with some sick designs. I have accepted that this is part of my life. I have also accepted some people cannot handle my honesty about this injury. So here's to breaking barriers and to show we are still sexy. Here's to confidence in imperfection. This may not be the most flattering post but as always I'm authentically me."

—social media post

By three years post-injury, the combination of finding a supportive community, curling, and participating in endurance events helped my confidence soar. My body was feeling good, and I had a giving-no-fucks attitude, which seemed to suit both my personality and my followers. Posing in a child's pull-up diaper was bold, shocking, and honestly a lot of fun. Anytime you can push against stereotypes of the physically disabled as shy, quiet, or off somewhere in the corner of the room is a good day.

What wasn't going so well was my Polaris GNCC sponsorship. Although I placed third overall in one race among a field of non-disabled men, I was there to finish, socialize, and feel a bit normal again, but not to win. On the way to the track, my routine was to

Confidently wearing a kid's pull-up diaper after losing 30 pounds gained after the accident.

My first wheel friend Chris—the inspiration behind the Wheel With Me Foundation—and me.

light up a joint to pump myself up and drown out both my thoughts and the chronic pain related to nerve damage from my spinal cord injury. Inevitably, that cannabis habit affected my performance too. It took the greatest tragedy in my life to make my dreams come true, yet I didn't fully appreciate it.

After three years, the team that maintained and traveled with the equipment abruptly dropped me before my contract with Polaris ended. Dropped due to an overall lackluster performance and a disagreement with the team manager about my cannabis use, I couldn't find another team, so my yearslong lifestyle of off-road racing ended.

I was curling pretty seriously by then and growing my brand, which pulled me away from the sport anyway, or at least that's what I told myself rather than admit to screwing up again. The story I told myself did have a nugget of truth, though. I had several other things to keep me busy, and GNCC racing often felt like a desperate attempt to hold on to my pre-injury life. I am forever thankful to my incredible sponsors for supporting me, but at that time my mind was weak

Competing at a curling competition.

and my newly paralyzed body wasn't ready to handle the competition. One constant in my life to that point was my lack of accountability. I still miss racing and hope to make a comeback someday. I believe I can compete again and finish well.

Before becoming paralyzed, I had never curled, but I knew the basics. Curling is traditionally a winter sport played on ice. In the warm climate of North Carolina, that means playing in an indoor club with an ice floor. Having watched curling on television, I knew players slide stone-like discs toward a target as in shuffleboard. Talking with actual wheelchair curlers, I discovered that wheelchair curling had become a para-friendly sport established as a Paralympic sport more than 15 years prior. That especially made my crazy competitive heart want to try it, intending to one day represent the United States on the Paralympic Team.

Coaches and teammates quickly got me up to speed on the particulars of the sport. Players slide curling stones of dense polished granite toward a target called the "house" or the bullseye on the other side of the ice. The stones are moved with a long-handled curling broom. I was set straight on the shuffleboard part: "Jesi, curling is more like playing chess on ice than shuffleboard. It requires strategy, teamwork, and skill. We will teach you the technique and scoring." After playing a few games, I was starting to get the hang of it.

When most people think of curling, they think of the sport where people run down and sweep the ice. Wheelchair curling doesn't have sweepers. We use a special stick that hooks onto the handle of the stone. You shoot the stone to the house on the other end of the ice from a stationary position. There are no sweepers to adjust the speed of the stone, so you have to be mindful of how the stone moves on the ice to understand its speed and then calculate how hard you will have to throw it. To me, the most attractive thing about curling is the technicality of the sport. My favorite thing was to smoke some green, get into my snow pants, and curl for hours, letting my mind work.

The USA Developmental Curling Team tryouts—or "trials," as they are called—were coming up. Getting a seat on the USA Developmental Team is the first step to making it on the professional Paralympic Team. Between attending curling camp and consistently practicing curling for a year, I was ready to go to trials. Deciding to attend trials was thrilling, but I knew I could not afford to pay for the amount of travel required to be on the team.

Since the accident three years prior, I'd been living in poverty. Both drivers involved— motorcycle and SUV—carried a minimum level of auto insurance. After my attorney fought hard, including looking for creative avenues, the final total payout was $100,000. From that, 30 percent went to attorney fees and 30 percent to health insurance fees, so my final settlement was around $30,000. That's a $30,000 total onetime payout to cover a life-changing injury that negatively impacted my ability to work and function daily. Having lived this nightmare, I will never go without quality auto coverage. Not only for myself but for anyone who may be impacted by an accident, my fault or not, where I am the driver.

If I wanted to do more with my life than feed myself, it was my challenge to find another way. My monthly Social Security disability checks were less than $18,000 per year, well below North Carolina's poverty line. I budgeted everything to the penny and did some under-the-table side hustles. My first obligation, which started day one at home from the hospital, was to pay my parents $275 a month in rent. After rent, there was transportation, clothing, food, and any medical-related needs not covered by Medicare.

After giving it a lot of thought, asking many questions of others, and diving into Google searches, I made one of the best decisions of my life. I started filling out grant applications and partnering with brands I used. I waited with high but guarded hope for my daily responses. Two grants came though, one from the Challenged Athletes Foundation and one from the Kelly Brush Foundation.

These two awesome organizations funded every aspect of my seat on the curling developmental team for not one but three years, renewing each year. My long-standing sponsorship with Kenda tires and a new sponsorship with Complete Care Medical also helped fund my curling and, eventually, Tough Mudder competitions. Collaboration and partnership are everything.

A few days before trails, I knew curling ice time was at a premium. I needed to schedule it and find someone to hold my chair while I tried to earn my spot at trials. I shared the story and made a plea for help on Instagram. The nicest guy—I'll call him The Nurse—responded, saying he'd be down to help.

Later, I discovered that this was a drunken, impulsive commitment, but that's another story.

The Nurse held my chair while I made the team. We started as friends, but I ended up dating that nice guy for two years. The Nurse, as his nickname implies, was not only a caring and skilled medical professional; he had it all. Looks, intelligence, a kind heart. He impressed me with knowledge of everything from history and current events to pop culture, geography, and sports. He also had a charming love for listening to full albums from beginning to end.

Curling put me on the road a lot of the time. With careful planning, I could affordably build in more opportunities in between curling events. Sometimes, I just had fun, like following the Arenacross Dirt Bike racing series in different cities with Taco. Other times I had obligations related to my increasing number of side roles such as being a brand ambassador and doing speaking engagements. For example, knowing we would be curling in the Cape Cod area, I scheduled my visits or work around the same time to help cover my travel expenses.

For the price of one night in a hotel, I booked a tent site at a KOA branded campground for a whole week, throwing my tent, sleeping bag, cooler of food, and camp stove in the car. Such campgrounds typically have an accessible bathroom and shower. I did the same thing during a curling trip to the Midwest, where another curler joined me and we split the campsite fee. Without these hacks, I wouldn't have been able to afford travel.

Rolling onto the ice for the first time as a developmental team member, wearing the USA jacket with my name on it, was pretty stinking cool. I got to represent my country. I'm proud and grateful to be an American. We live in a country that offers many opportunities, which makes me pretty fortunate. In some countries, people in my situation don't have access to basic medical supplies, therapies, or a wheelchair.

When I was dating The Nurse, he gave me a five-star experience everywhere we went. He did that with a lot of things. He took my dog on hikes when I traveled. Instead of appreciating and enjoying it, I found his constant attention irritating. The spark just wasn't there. After the honeymoon period, he took digs at me, especially about my lack of a degree. I don't know if it was intentional or not, but he regularly pushed me to my edge with subtle criticisms. Instead of communicating openly and trying to manage the situation constructively, I acted out by being ungrateful and unkind. When that didn't work, I tried other tactics. "Someone will love you the way you deserve, but it's not me. I think we should break up." He responded by talking me out of it. "Jesi, I love you so much. I can't lose you. Let's keep trying. We are good together."

I knew The Nurse wasn't a bad guy; he just wasn't the type of guy for me. Taking the immature route, I sabotaged the relationship by cheating with two other guys. After the first guy, I told The Nurse. We cried together, and he decided to stay in the emotionally unhealthy relationship. "Jesi, I just want you. I love you. We're not breaking up." It never occurred to us to set boundaries. Unmanaged, the situation escalated, dragging us away from who we were to a point where we lost ourselves. One day, as we pulled into the driveway of my parents' house, he started taking his usual digs at my intelligence. Fire rose inside as I blurted out, "I just want to hit you now!" He shouted back, "Go ahead. Hit me. HIT ME!" I hit him.

For sure I had some shitty qualities in how I treated men. Sometimes, I treated The Nurse like my personal assistant, which he pointed out a few times. I didn't want to be dating in the traditional, healthy, committed sense. I was looking to check in on the sensation in my lady parts and move on. I hate that I treated him the way I did; he did not deserve that, but old habits die hard, and using others was a hardwired habit, something I did without forethought about the consequences. I cannot tell that man "I'm sorry" enough. I'm not going to sugarcoat my behavior towards The Nurse. My behavior was terrible. I was stuck in the mud of believing dependency on another person was a weakness. Weaknesses I wanted nothing to do with; I was all about toughness and independence. That was my brand.

As my relationship unraveled, things went pretty well on the curling front. Knowing there would be drug tests coming up and that a positive test would mean not participating for two years, I quit smoking cannabis three weeks before trials. Taking a drug test was no joke. On the day of my test, the woman came into the stall with me to watch me catheterize. I happened to be on my cycle at the time, so she watched me change my tampon. Talk about getting personal.

One of the coolest things about curling is the curling clubs.

Seattle, Washington, was my favorite. The curling ice was an old, historic, barely accessible club, but a memorable structure with its wooden character and friendly club members. In Phoenix, Arizona, I remember the incredible kindness of the people and the number of wheelies. The club in the greater Minneapolis area was a fun place to practice. The people at the Cape Cod club instantly made you feel like family. People who invited you in with open arms. It is an incredible community to be a part of. Curling taught me a lot about careful communication, too, which is required on the ice. It gave me incredible experiences and yet, once again, my shoddy performance allowed a golden opportunity to slip through my fingers.

I never did make the national team. After four years of training and competitions, I decided to stop curling. I love curling, and it wasn't an easy decision, but my shoulder integrity had started to deteriorate. I couldn't throw the stone without feeling pain, negatively impacting my performance. The biggest lesson I learned during my time in the program was to practice the way you play in competitions. Give it your best always. I wasn't making the national team because I wasn't practicing the way I competed in trials. I smoked cannabis before I came on the ice during practice, but when trials came around, I was sober. Practice the way you play. Everything can impact your results.

18

What Is Love?

The Nurse and I had a lot of tender moments. One of those times was when some of my spinal hardware cracked. Of course, I didn't know what happened at first, but my back was persistently sore and there was a clicking noise when I moved back and forth. This was enough to prompt a rare trip to urgent care; I asked them to take an X-ray of the area. That's when they found out that one of my rods had completely broken in half and that the lower two screws were also broken. The doctors weren't too surprised, assuming it cracked because of my limit-pushing lifestyle. They reminded me I was a lot more active than their typical spinal cord injury survivor.

At my medical consultation, I was given three options: remove and replace, repair, or do nothing. Doing nothing was out of the question. Besides pain, the break was positioned in a way that the open space rubbed together when I moved, making a pretty loud noise. That noise was driving me insane. My doctor didn't want to remove or replace it because the crack was connected to a large amount of hardware. I reluctantly agreed to a repair job, feeling skeptical. *What if it happens again?* Part of me wanted everything out and to start over, but ultimately I agreed to a repair mostly because I didn't want the complicated aftermath of a complete replacement.

Once I made my decision, I told The Nurse, with fear in my eyes, "They are going to have to operate. Cut my back open, repair the broken hardware, and close it back up." The Nurse, who was by then extremely busy working full-time as a nursing assistant and very shortly set to graduate and start his first demanding registered nursing job, without hesitation replied, "That's okay, babe. We are in this together, and I will take care of you."

I signed up as soon as I could and just went for it. Less than a

18. What Is Love?

Just a girl and her best friend tending to our garden at home.

month later, I reported to surgery to fix the cracked rod and remove the lowest level of broken screws. I entered the hospital thinking: *The funniest joke you can tell God is your plan. Here we go.* Surgery is not what I wanted, but I was excited to get the crack fixed and get back to normal life.

When my groggy self came out of surgery, I was greeted by not just any nurse but The Nurse. The next day was his first day on the job as an RN in the same hospital. I wasn't expecting to see him off duty waiting patiently in my hospital room. After his long shifts, he lovingly cared for me in the hospital, even staying with me during the following days after becoming a newly minted registered nurse. He continued to care for me at home during the recovery weeks that followed. It was a slow, lonely road to get myself back to wellness. I persevered by setting small goals and working day by day to get better.

Trying to stay positive, I posted an upbeat post while offline I began the slow road to recovery:

"I never planned to go under the knife again, but damaged hardware called. The surgery went well. The first night not so much. The incision pain brought me to tears every time I moved ... but we are persevering! THANK YOU to everyone who sent well wishes. After 7 days I get to go home. I am beyond excited to see my husky, my bed, and to take a shower! I had PT the last two days; I was able to stand! I'm excited about the opportunities this hospital stay has brought me!"

After I fully recovered, my relationship with The Nurse lingered on for another year. Eventually, too much resentment built up. We agreed it was time to break up. There was simply not enough mature love to hold us together. Ultimately, our relationship wasn't all bad outcomes. Some good things happened, like being inspired to go back to school. Never really feeling good enough for him intellectually, I went back to school and finished my associate's degree after starting it eight years prior. I'm pretty proud of that piece of paper.

Months after the breakup, my shoulder started hurting so bad it limited my range of motion so much I had to adjust my furniture. The Nurse was the one who showed up to lower my bed. He also showed up when I needed help hanging my curtains. Even after I hurt him, he still showed up. After the breakup, I began missing him. Not the things he would do for me, but the intimate way he would say "Jes" when I would be acting like a lunatic or flying off the rails, how much he loved—truly loved—my dog Roxanne even when she was being sassy like her mom. I became so sentimental after the relationship ended yet had been ice-cold during it. My head was spinning. *Why now? Why couldn't I have appreciated him when it truly mattered?* Eventually, I decided to stop beating myself up with regret and self-loathing. Instead of wishing for parts of the past back, I decided, it was time to grow up.

They say men mature more slowly than women do, but that's a lie. Or maybe it was my spinal cord injury that delayed my social and emotional maturation. I prided myself on being a better person after the injury than before it, but I was anything but that in my relationship with The Nurse. It hurt my heart that I could treat someone so poorly, that he was so in love that he let me. I promised myself I would take the lessons from this and work to be a better me. I wanted to treat people with kindness, love, and respect. I wanted people to feel kindness, love, and respect. I knew the type of person I wanted to be. I just didn't know how to leap.

18. What Is Love?

Until then I hadn't done much to grow from the person I had been. My idea of a romantic relationship didn't include concepts of total trust, give-and-take, or intimacy. It was about using each other. Before the accident, I used guys for attention, sex, or gifts. After the accident, I used guys for physical help and, again, my attention-seeking bottomless pit.

When I decided to talk about the breakup and my regrets surrounding it with my Wheels2Walking influencer friend, he told me to list exactly what I wanted and didn't want in a relationship. I made that list. It was long. It felt unrealistic, so I buried it deep in my notebook. I decided to focus solely on myself. I became cold to love and the idea of spending life with another person.

As I pondered spending time truly alone, the pandemic hit, which was super convenient. At first, I thought of myself as a "compromised health person" who needed to be isolated, but soon I realized that my spinal cord injury didn't make me any more or any less prone to catching Covid. Still, with the world shut down, the timing was right for me to spend a rare extended amount of time without a partner or romantic flings. I went through a couple of nine- to 12-month periods without contact with the opposite sex—no touching, not even a date. I decided to do this because I had been a serial dater my entire life. I hopped out of one relationship right into the next. I didn't understand the power of human connection and sex to provide long-lasting, fulfilling happiness. Adding to that, being completely honest here, after I became a paraplegic, I had zero sensation in my vagina. That certainly didn't help my limiting mindset of sex solely being about penetration.

During these periods of complete celibacy, I journaled, reflecting on who I was, who I wanted to be, and how I wanted to impact the people around me. Yet, especially at first, I was bitter. Other people's happiness in their relationships got under my skin. I didn't believe their love and happiness. I gave my friend a hard time about her relationship with a wheelchair-using boyfriend. I repeatedly stated how I could never date another wheelchair user. I kept bringing up how I could never be with someone in our situation. Doing so, I was talking down on her relationship, projecting what I wanted on her. In a moment of clarity, I thought, *Who am I to dictate how someone else lives her life? Could this be more than that? Perhaps it is a reflection of my unhappiness being on my own?* I decided to stop judging my friend and everyone else about how and whom they chose to love. To treat others as nonjudgmentally as I hoped to be treated in my next relationship.

Amid deep introspection, I found myself chasing demons while attempting to discover for the first time what it means to truly love and accept yourself. Finding self-love in a body out of your control is frustrating. And it wasn't the paralysis that caused this; I'd struggled with self-love at least since I hit puberty. While I'd dated a few guys seriously, I'd rarely been faithful in my relationships. It wasn't that I didn't care about who I was with, it's just that I was always looking for something better. I looked for all of my validation as a worthy person from male attention. When I got it, I felt high and powerful. Perhaps I knew on some level I was out of control, but on another, I didn't care. I did what I needed to do to get the next fix.

Expanding my quest for self-love, I got to know my own body. To get there, I had to be willing to experiment with different toys and positions by myself. This was the most awkward part for me; it always had been. But the more comfortable you are alone, the more confident you are with a partner. The result was gaining more confidence in myself.

A confidence that shines through, especially in the bedroom. I also learned that there are different paths to orgasm that trump penetration. Disabled individuals are sexual individuals. We need that human connection to feel whole, just like anyone else. But, disabled or not, before we can give ourselves to another, we need to dive deep on our own. Now, I have no problem redirecting my partner if the experience is anything but pleasurable. We cannot expect people to know what it takes to get us going instinctively. Because of my limited sensation below the waist, foreplay is everything. Hitting the neck, ears, nipples, and lips with different sensations throughout the experience is very helpful in becoming aroused.

I learned I don't need someone else to be great. I have my person, and that's me. I can give myself everything I need. I can be by myself. I don't need praise, I don't need reassurance. I celebrate myself every day and choose to share that with the world. But a partner would be a nice addition to this bubbling-up self-love. I'm letting God guide me the way he does through this massive lesson of *trust in the process.* I didn't start recovering from my injury until I began to love my body. Rather than focusing on regaining the lost function, I focused on being the healthiest, happiest version of myself. Recovery came with that, and maybe love would work out in the same way.

All in all, quarantine was extremely good for me. I became more productive on my brand than ever. And I started to love myself and truly not give a single fuck what anyone has to say about me. I knew my heart. I knew my mission. I knew my God. I had my loved ones' support. I even did something I had never done. I joined a pandemic-related protest. For me, getting vaccinated wasn't the right decision. I didn't agree with the emerging laws that limited my access to places for making that choice. A year prior, I would never have dared say or do something controversial in public. I would have never stood up for something I believed in. The pandemic helped me find my confidence in my beliefs. Discovering self-love was empowering me and took me from follower to leader.

Reflection

I still don't understand why I thought the way I did or acted the way I did towards men. To those I hurt along the way, I'm truly sorry. I was a broken girl creating broken men. My intention was never to hurt you because I wasn't even thinking about you. I was thinking about what I could gain from you, along with a quick hit of pleasure.

During my celibacy periods, I was lonely for sure. I longed for a partner. Someone to share my drive, my success, my life. A person to hold me with love. Reassure me when I'm full of doubt. A team where we could support each other while we build our dreams. To live a limitless life. A life of arguments followed by laughter. Support, passion, and compassion. Respect and drive. My best friend.

Yeah, I wanted a partner, but I was also so freaking DONE with idiots who treat me like I'm second-class. My time is valuable, and I'm done wasting it. I'm starting to realize the type of person I truly want. I've gotten very clear about my nonnegotiables and desires.

I have so much love to offer; I want someone to appreciate it while reciprocating it. I don't want to say I'm sad overall because life is going pretty well, but I have a longing and an emptiness to build a life with another person and maybe even have kids one day. This is the one part of life I have yet to master. But I'm enjoying the in-depth lesson on patience even when I'm not enjoying it at the moment. I'm also enjoying the in-depth lesson on personal development as a whole. I have to be the quality of person I desire to spend my life with. I must be the type of person I want to attract.

19

Peaks and Valleys

"Life is truly peaks and valleys.
Some days I'm super grateful for the way I get to
experience life, other days I've pissed myself 3 times
before lunchtime, my legs feel like they are on fire, my
spine feels like it's coming through my skin, my hips feel
dislocated, and I'm unsure of every ounce of my being.
The key is LETTING MYSELF FEEL ALL OF THE
FEELINGS WITHOUT JUDGEMENT. I then allow
myself to move on from them by reminding myself of all
I have to be grateful for.
Regardless of your obstacle, ask yourself how much
control you have over this situation & what I could
learn from this experience. If you have no control over
something, don't let it control you & there is a certain
strength in our ability to grow. Sending love to you
guys. Know you're not alone. #wheelwithme"
—social media post, five years post-accident

As the pandemic lingered on, physical weakness snuck up on me
a little each day until I couldn't transfer strongly. My normal activities of daily living include getting from my bed to my wheelchair,
going to the bathroom, and getting dressed. These tasks suddenly felt
like huge physical feats. My shoulders, which take a beating every day
(as any wheelchair user can tell you), were constantly sore. More sore
than at any time in the past. In short, I kept doing my activities, but
overall I was struggling, feeling like crap most of the time.

A few weeks into this physical decline, my back started making a
creaking noise accompanied by pain. I went to the neurosurgeon for
a consultation and X-rays. He dismissed my concerns. "Jesi, I can't
see anything wrong with your hardware. Take it easy for a few days

and you should be fine." Three years later I would learn that I wasn't fine. There was an undetected crack in my hardware, but, being misdiagnosed, I pushed through the noise and pain by staying active and busy.

Feeling poor physically took a toll on my mental health. I was in chronic pain, and I was not happy. Often, it was hard to think beyond physically getting through the day. And just when I thought things couldn't get worse, I woke up to tragic news. My cousin was dead, our family's second close relative to die by suicide. My oldest sister's daughter passed away just a year prior. We were crushed, and, as a family, we grieved hard. While grieving, I felt a familiar feeling. An all-consuming jealousy. The same jealousy I felt when my niece took her life. A jealousy that they no longer had to feel pain. Jealousy that their battle was over. I started telling myself: *You have a choice. You don't have to deal with this shit.* Tears streamed down my face as I fought my internal battle. Then, out of nowhere, a competing thought: *It's time to give up control and put God in charge.* Clinging to this thought like a drowning person with a life buoy, I folded my hands and prayed: *God, I have no idea why I am here. I am giving my life to you. I trust that you have a plan for me. I'm sad. I'm lost. I want to give up this anger over my paralysis. I need your guidance. As I put myself in your hands, I have faith that these dark days won't last. Take my life and do your will with it.*

It was a simple yet profound act that I took seriously. I begin praying regularly and reading scripture and devotionals. I started keeping a Bible in my car to open and read when I needed inspiration. I prayed and listened to worship music. I filled my head with God. Instead of spiraling into dark thoughts, I leaned into God for strength.

Shortly after I gave my life to God, a friend introduced me to a company called 1st Phorm. She gave me a jug of their protein powder to try. Pumpkin spice is a flavor I've always been crazy about, so, naturally, I loved it. Getting more acquainted with 1st Phorm, my friend informed me they were doing an athlete search. I applied and was selected to be a guest attending 1st Phorm's first "outsiders" trip to their new headquarters in Fenton, Missouri. I felt super energized after rolling onto the 1st Phorm corporate campus for the first time. Suddenly, I was surrounded by dozens of like-minded people who shared my passion for fitness. I thought, *Yes, these are my people. This is where I belong and an environment to help me become the best version of myself.* We worked out together, talked about nutrition, and met the owner of 1st Phorm and author of *The Book on Mental Toughness* and *75 Hard*, someone I'd long admired and followed.

At one of the 1st Phorm dinners, I explained to an experienced representative about my gradual but significant physical decline. After I described my symptoms, he said, "Sounds like you aren't eating enough protein. Have you thought about tracking your nutrition?" This was an aha moment, the first time I connected food and its impact on the pain we experience in our bodies. It makes sense, but it isn't common sense. His advice and the impact of that entire weekend experience stayed with me.

> To the entire 1st Phorm team and my fellow athletes THANK YOU. I am feeling overwhelmed with gratitude and positive vibes! Your hospitality, perspective, knowledge, and expertise have me stoked to get after it! I left the weekend recharged, refocused, and ready to go. Thank you for showing me what it means to be a part of the 1st Phorm *#phamily!* Until we meet again, so much love to you guys!
>
> —social media post

I started tracking my nutrition to be sure I was eating the proper amount of protein, carbs, and fats to support my body's goals. When you don't eat enough, specifically not enough protein, your muscle repair may become difficult because muscle is created from protein. When you don't eat enough protein over a long period, your body may begin to break down the muscle you have to support other functions that need protein. Getting quickly into tracking, I realized I wasn't eating enough protein, averaging only 30 to 60 grams a day. Upping my protein significantly and consistently for a few months, I saw real results! Transferring was easier! Muscle soreness lessened! I was more independent!

Building my body on the outside with weights and on the inside with healthy food, I began an in-depth study of nutrition that included ongoing training through 1st Phorm's education platform. Learning to manage nutrition helped me learn to manage life. Not only was it a great physical feeling, but emotionally I felt more level and in control. Something super important not only because of my physical challenges but also the associated emotional ones, including severe adult attention-deficit/hyperactivity disorder, depression, anxiety, and a brain injury. Ailments I was learning are pretty common for so many people.

Inspired and on fire, I took a deep dive, learning as much as I could about the power of food and becoming a nutrition coach to help others. Over time, I completed my level one nutrition coaching certification through the Nutritional Coaching Institute. It was fascinating to learn how we can make nutrition work for us to contribute to our longevity and wellness. Food truly is power regardless of your physical abilities or goals. I became an affiliate for 1st Phorm as an advisor for their app and took all of the online nutrition courses they offer. I read and did more self-study then moved on to 1st Phorm coaching to help others.

Once I got my nutrition on point, good days started outnumbering the bad ones. I had more hours in the day because I wasn't physically struggling. While the world came out of the pandemic, I was coming out too. Literally out everywhere as a guest on two monthly podcasts for three years straight. Podcast appearances built up a significant social media following. Podcast interviews are my favorite because they allow me to share my platform with other creators and enjoy fun collaborations.

To prepare for podcasts, I reflect on practical messages to help listeners. Early on, my focus was on practical things to know. Things I learned the hard way. For example, the message to invest in good vehicle insurance and motorcycle helmets. You never know what the future might bring. I found I had a curious, able-bodied audience interested in my perspective as a wheelchair user, so I shared freely and enjoyed giving others a glimpse into my world. Later on, as I accumulated more knowledge about fitness and living a life of integrity and purpose, my messages became more philosophical.

Traveling and joining many activities also provided content to build my platform. "Frustration of Paralysis" helped but wasn't the catalyst that moved me into influencer status. It was me being raw, real, and honest. I went live online when I was happy and sad. I posted often, sharing my emotions and staying authentic, working hard to use the voice God gave me to motivate, educate, and hopefully make the world a bit better.

In addition to podcasts and being genuine, I used other tactics to grow my media platform. Standard practice or commonsense strategies that work. I went to pages of people who shared similar interests, liked or followed their pages, and interacted with their followers. I also stayed consistent and diligent with my own social media posting.

One day, five years after my accident—years spent putting serious effort into social media—a little blue verification check mark appeared on my Instagram. This status resulted in more and more brand partnerships. One of those was from Disney, and it was for their movie *Jungle Cruise*. They asked me to do a *Jungle Cruise*–themed workout, so I went up to the mountains of North Carolina. I made this whole workout independently, naming the movements around the movie. As a reward, I got early access to the movie, which was so cool. Watching the film, I noticed Disney had imprinted my name across the screen. This was meant to prevent me from pirating or selling the film. Something about seeing my name on the screen grabbed my attention. It was the very first moment I thought, *Wow. If I caught a huge company like Disney's eye, maybe my social media platform could grow enough to make money while helping people.*

20

Elevator Effect

*"Each friend represents a world in us, a world possibly
not born until they arrive, and it is only by this meeting that a new world is born."*
— *Anaïs Nin*

Despite physical and emotional setbacks, Wheel With Me
never left my heart. Taco gave us the name, Justified Cultures owner
Dundee made everything possible, and my friend Chris gave us the
mission. Chris is a special friend I met during my inpatient stay at
the rehabilitation center. Chris was injured when he was 50. A lively,
interesting guy full of stories, we were rehab buddies despite our age
difference. Both of us were spinal cord injury survivors, but I happened to be that unicorn patient whose parents already owned an
accessible apartment in the basement of their house. Chris, having
nowhere accessible to go, had to choose the only remaining option,
which was nursing home placement. When this happened to Chris,
I felt frustrated. This shouldn't have been his only option. We could
do better, and who better to teach, mentor, and support newbies to
wheel life than those who have lived it?

Long-term, Wheel With Me Foundation's mission is to create
transitional housing for new wheelchair users between rehabilitation
center stays and independent living. A residential setting staffed by
experienced wheelchair users who can mentor the newbies on how
to live independent lives. Independence through mentoring in practical matters like wheelchair skills, securing accessible long-term
housing, managing household tasks required to live in that housing,
employment coaching, and any other needs or gaps.

Thinking about Wheel With Me and the incredible people who
are now a part of it reminds me of the elevator effect. When you get

Nikki (right) and me posing for our app Wheel With Me Adapt Fit.

on the elevator, frequently it's empty. Where do you place yourself? Typically, it's in the front, centered at the doors, and ready to exit when the doors open. The selfishness of human nature never considers the high probability that regardless of what side of the doors you are on, someone else will want to get on or off that same elevator. Meaning you are in their way. It doesn't even cross our minds to consider that someone else may be using the elevator. There are a lot of lessons on selfishness, consideration, and mindfulness we can learn from an elevator. Consumed by our internal and external worlds, we don't expect anyone else to be on the other side of those elevator doors when we use them. I'm careful to wait off to the side these days, just in case.

Before my accident, I was that person standing square center in front of the elevator doors, waiting for them to open, with no thoughts of anyone being on the other side. I never considered that the unexpected could happen to me. Yes, I had friends, and overall, I did like helping people. For example, I helped my patients improve their confidence with a straight smile at the orthodontic clinic. Yet, it never occurred to me to go out of my way to consider others' needs enough to volunteer or serve outside of paid work, to move over and give someone room to jump off or on the elevator.

Getting hurt and becoming that vulnerable person who needs help sometimes gave me the gift of empathy. Gratitude for being helped has a way of upping your game. You seek out opportunities to be the helper because you are humbled by all the help you've received. You don't need to be disabled to get there, but you do need to go against those selfish instincts that are deeply ingrained in all humans. It feels damn good too.

Once the Justified Cultures owner "retired" from her volunteer position with the Wheel With Me Foundation, I started searching for help running the nonprofit website and my nutritional consulting business page. I didn't have the bandwidth to do it all. I put a simple Snapchat story out asking for help. The sweetest woman, Jackie, who happens to have spina bifida, responded. "I'll take the job." I didn't have much to pay, but she didn't care about the money. She cared about the mission of supporting wheelchair users to independence. Jackie was very hardworking in her quiet, unassuming way. She rolled into position full force.

A few months later, we discussed the idea of an "Empowerment Week" where we'd have members of the wheelchair-using community virtually share their skills or trades to show other members of the community what was available to them. Jackie helped get the presenters, and then we put on the event every evening for one hour for five days. It was a hit! We started doing Empowerment Weeks every quarter.

Empowerment Weeks were not the Wheel With Me Foundation's original vision, yet they have become the core of our work and align perfectly with its mission to help build independence for wheelchair users. They give us a financially achievable focus, and I learned something about being flexible and how where you start isn't always where you end up. The focus of Empowerment Weeks is on growth and development through independent skill building. Participants learn from the presenters and one another. We also have community meetups.

At the meetups, we socialize and share information in an informal setting. In recent years we've co-hosted an annual outdoor retreat focusing on whole body health through accessible adventures designed to push the bounds of independence. It's a "push" that comes with loving kindness from physically disabled peers rather than the medical community or a model.

Who better to teach wheelers than other wheelers?

As the Wheel With Me Foundation grew with the help of Jackie's efforts and I became more occupied with nutritional coaching, it was clear that we needed an operations manager. Just as Jackie and I came to this realization, we met this incredible woman at one of the Empowerment Weeks: Brianna—or Bri, as everyone calls her—from Black River Falls, Wisconsin. Bri and I are close to the same age and share a similar outlook on life and a passion for helping others. Having clicked at Empowerment Week, Bri asked if I would be her nutritional coach, and of course I agreed. "Oh, hell yes. That sounds like fun."

Bri worked hard and became my superstar client, modifying her diet to lose 30 pounds in addition to 70 pounds lost on her own, totaling 100 pounds down. Bri's generous heart simultaneously jumped in to work with Jackie and me on Wheel With Me projects. Bri was in school planning to become a social worker, and it didn't take much time before my nutrition coaching relationship with Bri morphed into a deep friendship.

As her graduation approached, I asked, "Bri, would you consider uprooting your life and joining me as the Wheel With Me Foundation director?" I had no doubt God brought Bri and me together. She was the person Jackie and I needed to join the Wheel With Me team. We tentatively planned to become roommates after she graduated from college. Our vision was to share living expenses while growing Wheel With Me together. We weren't sure where we would live but we had fun discussing all the possibilities.

I was working with both Jackie and Bri remotely when a fitness application developer (who noticed my social media work) cold contacted me via email. He encouraged me to consider launching a fitness application just for wheelchair users. I thought it was another spam marketing scheme, so I ignored the emails. Then, he became persistent and routinely checked in despite being ignored. This went on for six months. Eventually, I had Jackie and Bri check him out. They spoke with him and reported back. "Jesi, he is the real deal. We think you should talk with him." Once on the phone, I realized he had a brilliant idea: expand the social media content I had already created into a first-of-its-kind phone fitness application for wheelchair users. We went for it.

Naming the app was easy—Wheel With Me fitness app. The tricky part was getting Jackie, Bri, and me together in the same physical space to create start-up content since we all lived in different parts of the country. Tackling logistics and fears, we planned to meet up in North Carolina for two weeks. I remember the excitement of picking them up at the airport. We couldn't stop looking at one another, smiling and laughing. The internet became real life.

Over those two weeks, not only did we create bomb content, but I also taught Bri how to use a catheter in the toilet. Previously, she only knew how to use one in bed, which meant several disruptions to her day, getting back into bed every time she had to pee. We also taught Jackie how to use a catheter independently, something she had never experienced.

This get-together for business turned into a big growth moment for all of us. I had to learn patience working with other wheelchair users who hadn't had the independent skills training that I had. When you have only yourself to worry about, it's much easier. As challenging as it was, when the two weeks were over we realized the extraordinary things we had accomplished together. It was one of those rare "wow" experiences you remember forever. Without consciously trying, we had brought the Wheel With Me Foundation mission— building independence through peer-to-peer residential-based coaching—to life. And it worked!

There was give-and-take, interdependency, trust, and respect throughout our time together. *Wow, who knew the same qualities I was trying to bring into future romantic relationships could exist in platonic relationships?* Bri and Jackie are high-quality, altruistic, and trustworthy friends. The kind of people who made me want to be better.

The Wheel With Me fitness app was a hit. We picked up subscribers at a steady pace and had fun collaborations creating content. One day, I received a message from a young woman named Nikki Walsh. Nikki was paralyzed in a car accident three years after I was. Nikki is this beautiful, vivacious blonde with a college degree in kinesthetics. Her interest in physical fitness started long before her accident when she worked one-on-one with clients as a personal fitness trainer.

At first, Nikki's messages were peppered with questions. She'd write, "Jesi, you're an inspiration to me. Tell me how you got fit." I'd respond to these messages, sharing my story and strategies, including nutrition. Nikki reminded me a bit of myself in her ability to connect and ask questions early on, and it was cool to be honored to have the opportunity to mentor someone so recently injured.

Our correspondence continued on and off for two years. Nikki progressed. A personal trainer before her injury, she dropped the weight she wanted to lose. She took an interest in 1st Phorm, joining me as a legionnaire—a product representative, that is—in the 1st Phorm affiliate program. That meant that Nikki and I connected more and more as she regained strength and re-established herself as a personal trainer under the rebrand Nikki Walsh Adapt Fit.

Then the messages took a turn. "Jesi, how did you start your fitness app? I really want my own fitness app!" I wanted to help Nikki, but I was worried. *Nikki is an experienced personal trainer. If she starts her own app, who will come to mine?* One morning, rushing out the door to work, I turned to Brianna, "Hell, I'm so nervous. If Nikki gets an app, we are screwed. So screwed, everyone is going to go to her app!" What I didn't know then was that Nikki had similar fears. *Oh man, it's my dream to have my app, but the Wheel With Me app is so established and so good, who is going to join mine? Why would they? They already have Jesi's app.*

Caught up in this comparison game, I'd fight back with the truth. *Our journeys are completely different. We are two different people doing two different things. Competition can be motivating.* This was how it went until I attended a nutrition coaching conference. Each year, they center the conference on a different theme. That year was all about collaboration. Everywhere I turned, whether in large groups or breakout sessions, everyone's message was collaboration. *You gotta collaborate.* Okay cool. So, I got the message loud and clear. After the conference, it was my turn to message Nikki: "Hey Nikki, you and I are going to work together. I don't know how, but I'm so excited." The word collaboration continued to swim in my head. Nikki had so much to offer with her physical training, education, and skills. We complemented each other perfectly, with her focus on physical activity and mine on nutrition and wellness. Nikki also had more time to devote to the app. I sent Nikki a message: "Hey Girl, Why don't we merge Wheel With Me with Adapt Fit into the same app?"

Nikki agreed, and we pooled our efforts rather than competing. Negotiations started, and we decided to get attorneys involved in our interests. Searching for an attorney, I found an awesome woman named Macy who happens to be a quadriplegic. She came highly recommended, and working together I learned she's a boss woman and attorney. She does not stand down and made me feel well-represented. This attorney became my anchor, working with my total business and helping me make well-thought-out decisions before acting. Another positive from this merger.

Wheel With Me Adapt Fit was born. We aimed to serve the wheelchair-using community of all levels needing adaptive fitness. Excellence was important to us, so we worked to the best of our ability. The coolest part of it all? Out of this partnership, moving over so we both could fit in the elevator, I got an incredible friend, a beautiful human who has made the app more than I ever dreamed it could be. Because of Nikki, we are more impactful and powerful. Nikki is better at fitness. Brianna is better at running a nonprofit. The best thing I ever did was take a step back, letting go of some control to let others do what they excel at. Collaboration truly does make us better.

As I grew in self-awareness, I started unfollowing people who made me feel "less than"—the ones I compared myself to. I unfollowed them not because they had done anything wrong but because something about their content negatively affected my emotions and mindset.

Reflection

God is my anchor now. I start choosing to eliminate anyone or anything counterproductive to being my best self. I begin to consciously speak to myself with kindness. Then, before speaking to someone else, I ask myself, How do I want this person to feel? What energy do I want to bring? *Selfish as needed for self-care but compassionate and considerate enough to give plenty of floor space on the elevator.*

21

Mental Toughness

*"Here's the deal, you are the problem. The good news?
You are also the solution."*
*—adage variously attributed to
pastor Harry Emerson Fosdick
and activist Eldridge Cleaver*

My friend Jamie introduced me to another friend, Amber Balcaen, the professional stock car racer who wrote the foreword of this book, and someone else who became an amazing friend. Around the same time I reached the six-year marker of being paralyzed, Jamie, Amber, and I decided to try a mental toughness challenge called 75 Hard, developed by 1st Phorm's founder Andy Frisella.

I was no stranger to mental toughness challenges. Endurance events, including ATV racing and especially Tough Mudders, helped me build all-important mental toughness. There's nothing more grit-inspiring than to be getting after it on a cold, wet, muddy obstacle course for 24 hours. Exhausted and uncomfortable to the core. In the middle of the quiet night, left with your thoughts, mindset is everything. Yet, mental toughness also requires mixing it up and challenging yourself in new ways. Someone can call you "confident" all day, but you won't truly believe it or embody it until you take action. Often I think about life as a game to keep beating the endless levels. We win at life one task at a time, and mental toughness is the foundation to do hard things.

75 Hard is a mental grit and development program. It's free, but I wanted the best results, so I downloaded the app to help me track and stay motivated. 75 Hard consists of five daily tasks, some stipulations, and zero compromise.

Part Three—Post-Accident

1. Do two 45-minute workouts daily, one outside, regardless of the weather. There's something about completing that outdoor workout in adverse weather (like rain or cold) that makes you feel unstoppable.
2. Drink a gallon of water daily. I kept my water by my bed so that as soon as I turned off the alarm, I could start hydrating.
3. Pick a diet and stick to it. I chose a whole foods–based diet with protein and calorie goals tracking macros in the 1st Phorm app. I also added supplements to fill the gaps. Join Team Wheel With Me to try it yourself (www.1stphorm.app/wheelwithme).
4. Read 10 pages of a nonfiction personal development book daily. Learning from another person's life experience can help you simplify your life. I recommend knocking this one out during your morning routine.
5. Take a daily progress picture. This one is about mastering the small details. How you do one thing is how you do everything. This is another task that is best done first thing in the morning.

Note: No alcohol or cheat meals. You must stick to the diet of your choosing. For me, that meant no fried foods or sweets, and tracking macros with a goal of hitting protein and calories. Once you start a book, you must finish it. You have to drink a full gallon of water. Protein shakes and drinks mixed with other things do not count. ONLY WATER.

We started together, and it went well until day 34. I was in a car accident that landed me in the hospital overnight. It was a weather-related accident. Roxanne and I were alone in my car, returning home from Jamie and Jimmy's house, and the sky let loose the worst sleet I'd ever seen. I lowered my speed, proceeding with caution. There was a truck behind me with his lights beaming in my mirror, so I switched to the far right lane. As he passed my front bumper, my steering wheel went fluid and I looked down the interstate through my driver's side window. I was attempting to correct the slide when my car spun out of control. I held on and rode the ride out. After banging the guardrail a couple of times, I shot across the interstate, finally coming to rest in the median. *Was Roxanne okay?* Every airbag was deployed, but my baby girl was lying on the seat, wondering what had happened. I called 911.

As the adrenaline slowed, reality set in. I'm paralyzed, I'd totaled my car, I was on the side of the interstate, and someone else could hit me. I held back tears and panic while the 911 operator assured me that help was on the way. *My first accident since THE ACCIDENT.* My sister Jodi with friends Johnathan, Jamie, and Jimmy jumped in to help me in my time of need. J team to the rescue.

That brief hospital stay cost me. I missed reading my 10 pages, one of the core requirements of 75 Hard. A quick lesson in the importance of knocking out tasks early in the day. The rule is that when you miss any of the requirements, you must go back to day one. So, not wanting to cut corners, three days after the accident I started all over again on day one. The second time I made it straight through to day 75. I finished my last day on the best day I could imagine, the day I was the maid of honor at Jessica's wedding. Jessica's wedding marked the end of an era in our lives. Our chatty calls about boys, going out together—all of those things were officially over. But it was a new beginning, too, with her new husband and stepson. I was excited and honored to be her maid of honor on such a big day. My best friend had been by my side on the day my life changed forever—my big day—and I got to return the favor for her.

The wedding of one of my curling friends also stays in my heart. The best man was another curler friend of mine who was tasked with giving the speech. This friend had a stroke when he was a teenager, so his speech isn't the best. He wrote his best man speech and practiced it repeatedly, but, in the end, he asked me to read it. He said I could read it in a way that would make the impact he wanted. Although he undoubtedly would have done it better, it was a beautifully written speech. It was a special honor for me and an example of the beauty of a trusting friendship.

As more supportive friendships came into my life, my confidence and social media influence grew. Everything fed off of everything else, leading me to become bolder in my efforts to connect with strong people, especially women.

A mutual friend introduced me to Chelsie Hill, a badass wheelchair-using woman making a difference for the community through dance. Once we were introduced virtually, I drove six hours from Phoenix to Los Angeles to meet her in person. To give you an accurate idea of how kind Chelsie is, she opened up her home to me for a few days even though we had only chatted on the phone. Chelsie founded the Rollettes, a wheelchair dance team. The Rollettes also offer group coaching through the Boundless Babes Society and a yearly meet-up called Rollettes Experience. I was excited to stay at her home but had reservations. Still a tomboy with my mostly makeup-free face and Tough Mudder, gritty, no-fucks-given attitude, how would I ever get along with a girly girl whose hair was styled to the nines, whose nails always looked fresh, and who enjoyed a perfectly polished Hollywood platform?

As it turned out, we vibed. Our mindsets, values, and goals were very similar. Chelsie, having over five years more business experience than I did, generously taught me several valuable business lessons during that trip. Lessons so ingrained in my mind that I still remember them. The first was not to sell yourself short. Brands, corporations, and others will often try to exploit you. With so many disabled people concerned about losing their benefits, they often get taken advantage of with companies giving them products for their time and commitment rather than payment. Chelsie told me, "You deserve more than poverty." Create a schedule and stick to it. Chelsie's days are very regimented and scheduled. It allows her free time with her husband, friends, and family. What brilliant advice. Once home, I implemented a disciplined schedule for myself using calendar blocking and committed to it. The last thing Chelsie reminded me was to remove the focus from you and place it on others. Work as a team and give back.

Friendship fosters so much enjoyment in my life. Still, the reality of the world and its bias and ignorance of my needs as a person with a spinal cord injury continue to confront me. Friends and my faith in God give me strength, but, sometimes, there simply is no shielding myself from life's tough realities. Occasionally, it's the simple annoyances. For example, when people notice me using my wheelchair in public, I can't say why exactly, but the sight of me as a young, otherwise healthy-looking woman in a wheelchair sets off alarm bells in some people's heads.

They practically trip over their own feet rushing in to do something for me. Like open a door or grab an item I am about to grab

Chelsie Hill, founder of the Rollettes Dance Team (right) and me.

myself off the store shelves. People also like to "help" by grabbing whatever I'm carrying on my lap to the cash register. I wish people would just let me do it. If I need help, I will ask. Otherwise, let me figure things out. Even if I do it a harder way than you would or if it makes you uncomfortable to see me struggle. A stranger's perspective that I, or anyone with a physical disability, perpetually needs help, words of encouragement, or any other form of unsolicited "support" is not my reality.

Early on after my accident, I would let tiresome comments ("Hey, speed racer! Look at you go!") or well-meaning but misplaced efforts of others to "help" affect me. After each encounter, my mood soured. Today I stand up for myself using hard boundaries to call out ignorance. Once, I was at a NASCAR race when a woman commented, "I'm going to let you go ahead of me so you don't run me over." I thought, *Run her over? No, I'm not letting this slide.* "What makes you think I would run you over?" Another time, at the gym, an older man asked me, "Why are you in that thing?" I calmly but firmly replied, "No." I don't owe anyone an explanation, nor should I allow anyone to bully me because I'm using a wheelchair. The wheelchair doesn't have to be a negative or a reason to perceive me as less than someone who doesn't need one. Before I was injured, I remember feeling sorry for one of my male patients at the orthodontic office who used a wheelchair. I thought his life was so sad, when in reality he lived life to the fullest. So, I get it. Yet I won't let others' misunderstandings about my disability affect me.

As my friends say, I just get it done. I don't care how ridiculous I look or if people stare with pity on their faces while I'm doing it. This attitude might look like I've toughened up. No. It's a softening. And understanding that others' discomfort and reactions to people with physical differences are out of my control and not intended to be hurtful—it's often just ignorance.

Empathy, hard boundaries, and sometimes humor. One day, years after my injury, I broke my driver's license in half. It was the same driver's license that was inside my jeans pocket during the accident, so it was already damaged. The break was inevitable. At the time, to get a replacement license, you couldn't just order one online. I went to the DMV in person. The representative glanced my way and then looked me up on her computer. She said, "I see you use a wheelchair. If that means you use hand controls, you need to retest to prove you know how to use them."

So, there I was with three years under my belt, driving adaptively, even driving across the country by myself, taking an adaptive driver's test with hand controls for the first time. My adaptive driving teacher, who told me I didn't need to retest, would be laughing if he knew. When it was time to back up, my hands were occupied with the hand controls, so instead of placing my right hand on the passenger's seat and looking over my right shoulder, I did an adaptive maneuver. I kept my hands on the controls and used my mirrors. The licensing woman began to panic. "What are you doing!?" I responded, "Would you be comfortable with me controlling both the gas and steering wheel with one hand or using my mirrors?" She chose the latter. I passed the driving test.

Taking my new license home, I glanced at it, noting that she had completely forgotten to include the hand control restriction.

21. Mental Toughness

By then, I was getting used to able-bodied people being pretty clueless when it comes to anything "adaptive." Instead of frustration, I try my best to keep a sense of humor and not make a big deal out of it. Experience has taught me that getting upset or feeling as though life isn't fair doesn't serve a good purpose. Life is life, and letting go of expectations has trained my mind to stay positive.

Yes, the Americans with Disabilities Act (ADA) was established over 30 years ago. A federal civil rights law, the ADA exists to prevent discrimination against disabled persons. For someone like me, that means, in theory, access to public places such as restaurants, airports, hotels, and recreation centers. I say "in theory" because there are caveats and exceptions. Also, places where ADA is disregarded. Adding to that, there are so many types of disabilities with their associated challenges. It's not realistic to expect people I encounter to understand all of them. Instead of complaining or feeling bitter whenever ADA isn't followed, I remind myself of the truth. It's not perfect, but we are decades ahead of many other countries when it comes to accommodating disabled persons. Still, to be disabled anywhere means you'll have to face barriers. You have to know when it's worth it to advocate for yourself and others. My moment was after an evening in Los Angeles, and it wasn't so much about ADA discrimination as it was about vaccine discrimination.

I was so impressed with Chelsie's mission that I attended the Rollettes Experience in Los Angeles, California. Events like the Rollettes Experience focus on bringing wheelchair users together to share, discuss pertinent issues, and socialize about how we cope with our challenges. Wheelchair-using women travel from all around the world to be part of this experience. It was an awesome event, except for what occurred outside of our protective event walls. A group of us were on the sidewalk near the hotel, and one friend fell hard on her face, knocking herself out. I looked up and understood why she fell. The streetlight was burnt out, and you couldn't see where the sidewalk ended. It was not marked. She had fallen face-first off a curb. Freaked out, we called the ambulance. Our friend was responsive before the ambulance arrived but confused and injured.

Terrified, my friend begged me to stay with her. I saw fear in her eyes. "Please don't leave me. Please don't leave me. Please don't leave me." I rode in the passenger seat of the ambulance. She rode in the back. Everything was cool until we reached the hospital, and I politely asked, "Can I go with her?" They asked for Covid-19 vaccination papers. Knowing damn well I wasn't vaccinated and couldn't fulfill the request, I replied that I didn't have them on me: "Hey, we were visiting from another state, this was an emergency, and my friend is very scared to be alone, especially vulnerable as a disabled person." The security guard shook his head "no" and pointed to a white event tent in the parking lot where I was to wait.

I had her wheelchair, identification, and medical insurance cards, and I made a promise to my friend, so I had to stay. Mind you, it was late and getting a little chilly, which can be torture for anyone with a spinal cord injury—I have poor circulation in my legs. It got colder and colder. Between the cold temperature, sitting too long in the wheelchair, and fears about being a young woman alone late at night in downtown Los Angeles, I was super uncomfortable. When I insisted, they found a nurse to update me. "Right now, we are trying to get her in a good place."

Hours pass, and it was 2 a.m. I had to use the restroom. Security said, "Ok, but come right back." When I returned, I noticed a gift. Somebody had made me a bed out of two chairs with a hospital blanket. I used my friend's wheelchair cushion as a pillow. My angel, another family member waiting on her loved one, helped position my feet. Normally I do not like receiving unsolicited help, but in this vulnerable circumstance, I was grateful and tried to sleep on my makeshift bed for several hours in the cold outside the hospital. Random people—some mentally ill, some battling addiction, some homeless, some all the these—walked through the parking lot. I was scared for my life. I am a paraplegic woman vulnerable to all sorts of dangers. Scared, I put my phone in my fanny pack, tucking it underneath me out of potential thieves' reach and for my easy access.

Sunrise. My friend called. "Hey girl, where are you at? Why did you leave me?" I said, "I'm outside. I have your wheelchair. I have everything. I've been out here all night." She couldn't believe I had to stay outside but was very relieved. They told her that she had come to the hospital alone, that no one was with her even though I had been there the whole time.

Of all places, you would think a hospital would be more sensitive to people's needs. Physically disabled people and their needs are not widely understood. The risk of something dire happening to me and spending a chilly night outside was far greater than the chance of me infecting someone. But it happened. Common sense crashing on the curb, just like my poor friend's body.

Nonetheless, I decided to use this experience to grow mentally tougher by email the hospital and sharing our experience. It's not easy to voice a complaint or know when it's worth it, especially when you are young and disabled. A lot of crap happens to us, and it takes strength to get through it at the moment and also to know what is worth the fight. They replied it was a miscommunication. "I am so sorry. It should never have happened that way. I will make sure this is addressed with our security staff." I sighed. My friend and I looked at each other and hugged. No words were needed.

Reflection

Off the streets of Los Angeles and back into the Rollettes Experience, I was treated to an auditorium of other beautiful women. We danced, laughed, and encouraged one another. Peer mentoring on steroids. Part of my life's work and focus is mentoring. Both as a mentor myself and getting mentored by others. Peer-to-peer mentoring is what the Wheel With Me Foundation is all about; it's what the Wheel With Me Adapt Fit app is all about, and it's the single reason I have a story to tell. Other people have been there to guide me. Nothing is done without a community of mentors. If I only had a single piece of advice to give someone, it would be to get yourself some mentors. If you can't find one in your community, go online. Go to the bookstore and read stories that resemble the person you wish to be. Accept that you will spend the rest of your life learning; we need each other to accomplish it.

22

Financial Freedom

"For 7 years I was terrified of getting off of Social
security disability
For 7 years I lived in complete poverty
For 7 years I lived in a limited reality
Work has FREED me from the chains of the system
Work FREED me from the limitations I created."
—*social media post after returning to work*
as orthodontic assistant

My definition of risk-taking is doing anything that makes you feel uncomfortable. It doesn't have to be athletic. It can be making a phone call, talking to a stranger, or doing anything for the first time. One of the biggest risks I've ever taken post-accident was deciding to go back to work as an orthodontic assistant seven years after my accident and six years after my first attempt trying and failing because I wasn't yet able to manage work and my disability.

I didn't come to this decision to return to work on my own. It took a family crisis. After visiting Chelsie in Los Angeles, competing in the World's Toughest Mudder, and visiting other friends in various parts of the United States, I returned to my parents' basement apartment. Instead of the usual travel gifts like a silly T-shirt or souvenir, I brought Covid home. I had no idea I had it. I just thought I was starting my period. It ran through the house. First, my mom got it. She got tested early on. Then, my dad contracted it. He didn't realize he had it until he felt super ill. He got so ill he was hospitalized.

One day from the hospital, Dad called my mom to tell her he wasn't sure he could recover from his infection. He was in my mom's ear, but the speaker was loud enough that I could hear the fear in his voice on the other end. "I'm not getting better. They are talking about

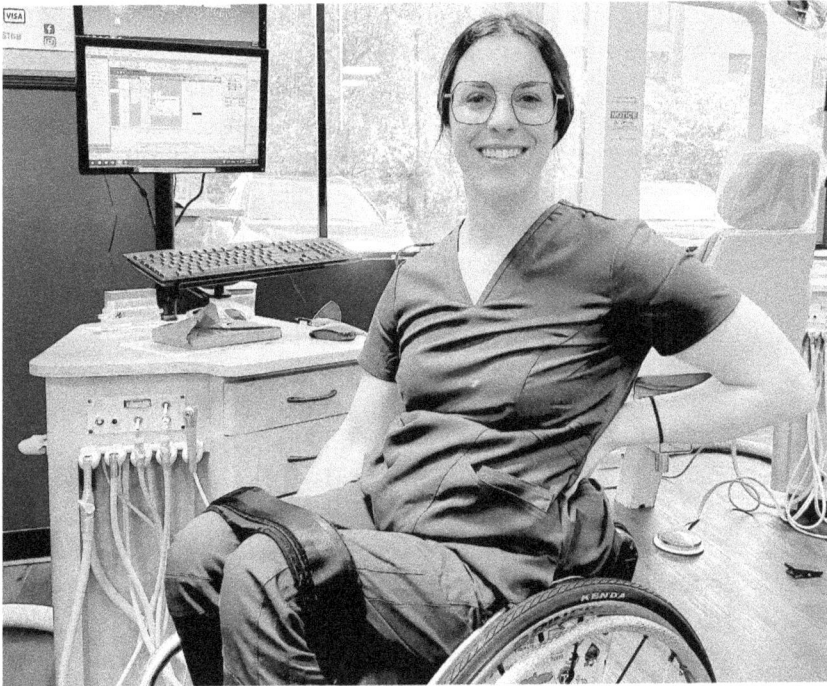

Back to work in my scrubs at the orthodontist office.

putting the tube down my throat. Don't let them put the tube down my throat. I don't want to die." Mom and I were terrified. He wasn't allowed visitors, so we had no way of directly advocating.

I started to think of the worst-case scenario. Something about experiencing trauma keeps you prepared for the worst, often taking your mind right there. The worst-case scenario was Dad dying. Without his income, there was no way Mom could keep the house. I would have to move out on my own, which wouldn't be possible in the Charlotte area on my poverty-level disability income, even with my side gigs of nutritional coaching, fitness apps, and brand ambassadorships. It simply wouldn't be enough. Dad eventually pulled through, but his health scare was a wake-up call. Nothing in life was guaranteed, including my housing. I needed to get a full-time job to earn enough to be able to move out someday. I also wanted to gain peace of mind that if something happened to either of my parents, I could take care of my dog and me.

Part Three—Post-Accident

By this point, Bri was preparing to graduate from college in Wisconsin. We talked more seriously about combining resources and moving in together. Perhaps together we could make it work on our disability incomes. We looked into several options, including moving to another state, but the tight housing market drove up the cost of rent. It was all out of reach and discouraging. My mom saw our struggle. "Jesi, maybe Bri should just move into our basement." We agreed. The best approach would be to stay put at my parents' house. I could get a full-time job, and Bri could manage things with Wheel With Me, keep the fitness app going, and support my journey back to work through teamwork on meal prep and household tasks. Of course, it would take patience and long-term thinking to make it work. For Bri, this was a huge step, and her life as she knew it was about to be uprooted. One day I got a call. Bri said, "Jesi, I'm ready. We can do this."

The thought of going back to work was terrifying. I imagine it is for a lot of disabled people. We are scared of losing our health benefits. We are scared of not having the stamina for a career, considering the extra hours each day needed to manage our physical disabilities. It took a long time to adjust to wheel life, putting myself in numerous uncomfortable places before taking that step. I found that with each smaller risk I took, my confidence grew. So did my independence. At this point, I was living in poverty. I had nothing saved. No nest egg ever, simply living with the stress of managing disability check to disability check supplemented by a few modest side hustles. Looking at the most successful disabled people I knew, they all shared a common theme of taking outside employment. I had no choice if I ever wanted to leave my parents' basement. I needed to save myself.

Considering my employment options, I knew my best bet would be to return to my former orthodontic assistant career. Even though it had been seven years since I had worked with a patient, this was my most valuable skill set. It was an in-demand career and something I enjoyed. I applied to 10 different places. Two offered interviews. I was hired at one. They wanted to complete their staff, and I was the perfect fit.

I was lucky. Putting on my scrubs for the first time in seven years was surreal. *I can't believe I'm going back to a day job.* I was scared but pushed through, motivated to succeed. The difference this time was that I had the physical conditioning and the confidence to hold my own. Working in that office would be tangible evidence of my progress. Then, one day, about a month after I started working, I received a letter from Social Security. They asked for pay stubs from the past three years! More letters followed.

I panicked initially, not knowing what to do before remembering Josh, an attorney who has a spinal cord injury and is a disability advocate. I'd met Josh while lobbying in Washington, D.C. When we met, he said, "Just reach out when you go back to work. I can help you with the financial aspects so you don't lose your benefits." So, I did. I scheduled a phone call with Josh on his booking link: https://bit.ly/Sp_Employment_WheelWithMe.

That phone call connected me to someone who helped me navigate a broken system. As a Ticket to Work Specialist, my advocate submitted documentation for me, communicated with the Social Security Administration, and told me about additional resources available, like an Able Account and the Medicaid buy-in program. Overall, she made the process a helluva lot easier than it would have been had I tried to navigate it on my own.

Over that obstacle and earning a paycheck for full-time work, I began building up a savings account for the first time since the accident. Tangible signs of my progress. I felt empowered and proud. Yet it was far from easy. Managing bowel, bladder, hydration, and other needs at work was nearly impossible. Adding to the challenge, the place was a shit show. The office manager who hired me and the doctor fought loudly in front of patients, daily. Patients frequently neglected to pay their bills, which forced me into the awkward position of refusing to treat them. In my opinion, shoddy work was being done, and our team was responding by dropping like flies. I continued to show up, doing my best to make the best of the situation. Plus, I loved the paychecks.

Bri was my anchor through all of these challenges. She was my anchor when I came home emotionally worked up. I wouldn't have gotten through that time if I hadn't had Bri. At the end of a long day, my brain was fried. I would make a sad attempt to communicate with Bri, but the words wouldn't come out right. I called this drunk brain because that's how my words sounded. Bri would reply, "Oh honey, your brain is scrambled." We'd smile, and I kept pushing on.

Part Three—Post-Accident

Throughout it all, I held firm to my values and morals. I didn't cut corners as I witnessed others often do. I strove to take the high road each day, a radical departure from my younger self who would have simply followed the crowd adding to the unprofessionalism and chaos. I even began adding extra fitness to my workday. For example, I put on my leg braces and walked with a walker during lunch breaks three days a week.

At first, it was hard. Just getting them on felt like a complete workout. Then, once they were on, progress was slow. In the racing world, there's a saying, "Sometimes you have to go slow to go fast." This was also true when adjusting to the leg braces. Each time I wore them, I tried little by little to do a fraction better than the previous time. Early on, that meant standing for a few seconds. Over days, weeks, and months, I progressed to walking slowly with a walker. I sometimes freaked my coworkers out by tackling the stairs with my wheelchair on the way to lunch.

My side hustles continued to grow and were bigger than ever. I also picked up a few opportunities to work as a brand ambassador for the Sweden-based company Wellspect. My relationship with Wellspect began in 2017 after I tried their LoFric brand of intermittent catheter and loved it. Wellspect is the company that manufactures the LoFric brand of hydrophilic intermittent catheters and Navina products for bowel management. Both LoFric and Navina are brands that I'm passionate about, so helping them locally was a natural fit.

I truly loved being a brand ambassador. I began considering how I could create a bigger impact and a more ideal employment reality for myself. One where I was more in my element as opposed to the orthodontist office, which no longer fit the person I became post-accident. I was meant to do more, be more. The orthodontist office increasingly had me feeling like a tiger in a cage, looking out through the windowed barrier separating me from serving my higher purpose. It was time to take a chance.

After six years in my role as brand ambassador, I proposed expanding my role at Wellspect into a full-time spinal cord injury specialist position. I envisioned visiting rehabilitation centers across the United States, sharing the company's story, including my positive experience with their products. I gathered the gumption to make the pitch by asking myself the classic question: *What is the worst that could happen?*

As Wellspect considered my proposal, I was busier than ever, trying to fit everything in. To make it work, I used strategies like calendar blocking. I scheduled everything, including my workouts. I silenced my phone. Discipline, a positive mindset, and hard work rewarded me. Wellspect agreed to my proposal. It slowly sank in. *I have my dream job and thousands of dollars saved in the bank. I'm working a full-time job for the first time in seven years and have a new job offer on the horizon. I am finally on my way to getting out of my parents' basement.* Then disaster struck.

23

Overtime

It happened on a typical weekday. I woke up and tried to sit up. There was a sharp pinching in the middle of my back. *That's weird.* I lay back down flat for a second, letting my back decompress. I got up, threw my legs off the bed, and transferred to my wheelchair. I felt it again, a sharp pinching. It hurt so bad. I was stuck with my upper chest kind of forward. *Why can't I sit up straight?!!!* Thinking it was morning tightness, I kept moving, pushing through the pain, hoping it would work itself out. I transferred to the toilet sloppily—it was more like a slide—because I could barely lift my body. I catheterized myself and managed my morning bathroom stuff to the best of my ability before sliding back into my chair.

Hoping a cold shower would help me loosen up, I transferred to the shower seat, having to slide again. I dragged myself onto the chair, showered cold, and prayed that my back would loosen up. I began to transfer back into my chair, but I was stuck. *What the fuck,* I thought, *how the hell am I going to get out of this mess?* Panic set in. Something was wrong, and I lost it. Pain radiated. I was sobbing.

After a few minutes of struggling, I composed myself enough to drag my body from the shower chair back to my wheelchair. With my spine still shooting intense pain and tears rolling down my face, I rolled to Bri's room, where she was already halfway into her chair. She asked, "What's wrong, honey? I heard you crying in the shower." I told her what was going on and that I was trying to get ready but had to let work know I'd be late. She told me, "You're not going to work today. You need X-rays. I know you. Something is wrong." I called work to let them know I wouldn't make it in for the first time in over a year. Defeat and fear washed over me like a giant wave. It's not that I can't swim when things get tough, but I wasn't expecting it. There is always the chance that wave will take you under; no matter how hard you try, it won't be enough.

Having been down that road once before, I had a suspicion of the cause: my spinal fusion. The numerous screws and two rods used to put my broken body back together in 2015, and repaired once since then, had probably cracked or broken again, causing the unbearable pinch. I texted my primary care doctor, asking if he could get me in for scans or if I needed to go to Urgent Care. A couple of hours later, I sat with him as X-rays proved I was right. Usually I love to be right, but this wasn't one of those times. The two rods had broken completely in two, slipping on top of each other rather than flush together. Misalignment caused pain and made me feel stuck. *Who knew I was a girl so strong she broke titanium twice?*

I was fitted for a large back brace to stop mobility. When they decompressed my T4 vertebra, they removed some of the protectants from the spine, plus the vertebra never healed properly. The X-rays confirmed the hardware crack I thought I felt three years earlier but the neurosurgeon said didn't exist. This crack was contributing to the pinching issue. Because of the nature of the burst fracture, without the hardware, my spine was not stable, putting me at risk of damaging my spinal cord and risking any return in function I had made over the previous eight years. Surgery was needed to remove the old fusion, replacing it a level higher and a few levels shorter because the lower fracture in my initial upper injury had healed.

Between this appointment and the one with the surgeon, I had an international trip to Sweden, where I was invited to deliver a keynote at Wellspect's global sales meeting. Going to Sweden was the coolest experience. I got to see how my catheters are made and meet the global team from all over the world. After that keynote, I started my trip back to the States but not before meeting Bri in Amsterdam for 36 hours of exploring and touring.

Amsterdam had always been a place I wanted to visit, especially because marijuana has been legal there for decades, which fascinated me. Wheeling out of the Amsterdam airport, we hailed a taxi to get to our hotel. Bri and I had booked an accessible room at the Marriott chain of hotels. The taxi driver shook his head in frustration while huffing and puffing in the pouring rain to get our luggage and chairs into his vehicle. We made it to the Marriott and were dropped on the corner. The taxi abruptly left.

Before we reached the hotel doors, the front desk woman greeted us: "We have a problem." Oh boy. The last words we wanted to hear after a long flight. She elaborated. "I'm so sorry, but the hotel is being renovated. We don't have an accessible entry during this time." Bri and I looked at each other. I explained: "We booked our accessible room two months ago through the Mariott app and called recently to confirm."

Bri and I stayed calm, and the hotel staff got busy finding another place for us to stay. While they sorted that out, we went exploring, rolling into what looked like a coffee shop nearby. Well, it wasn't a coffee shop. No, this was a pot pub, where, instead of drinks flowing, there was smoke blowing. Zero alcohol, just a place to smoke a joint and chill with your friends. For someone like me who doesn't drink alcohol but needs to relax, this was the bomb and more than I could have wished for at that moment. High people generally are calm and peaceful as opposed to binge drinkers. The atmosphere put us in the best headspace to deal with the hotel mishap.

We checked into our next hotel, and the room was perfect with a roll-in shower and everything. Wasting no time, we hit the streets on our wheels, taking in the stunning architecture of this 700-year-old city. It was breathtaking. The canals are steep, and we laughed struggling to get to the top, enjoying the quick burst of wind in our hair as we went down the other side. We rolled by the famous Holocaust-era Anne Frank House. Gawked at the beautiful cathedrals. We even enjoyed McDonald's in Amsterdam because why not? Amsterdam turned out to be the perfect mashup of New York City feel with an anything-goes Las Vegas vibe. A trip I could only have done with my ride-or-die Bri.

Returning front my overseas trip, I saw the surgeon. He reassured me that the surgery would be easy-peasy. After removing the old hardware, they would put thicker rods in my spine to hold up against my active lifestyle. I'm not a normal post–spinal fusion individual. He gave me clearance to use the barbell again as long as I wore the back brace while waiting for surgery. I had my typical summer trips planned: 1st Phorm's Summer Smash, The Wheel Together Retreat, and Rollettes Experience, landing me right into the end of summer for surgery.

Three weeks post-operation, I had a keynote in Baltimore, Maryland, planned. I wasn't sure I would be ready to make the trip, but it was important to me. I was scheduled to present to professionals who help people with disabilities navigate the complex Ticket to Work Program. The Ticket to Work Program helps disabled people transition off Social Security disability payments by protecting their benefits while they work for the first several months. Once established, Ticket to Work recipients can earn an income without losing medical benefits. In my case, working qualifies me for MORE medical benefits, including full North Carolina Medicaid. I didn't qualify for Medicaid when I received monthly Social Security disability payments! I got to work my way out of poverty and have medical coverage. *Heck yes!*

The Ticket to Work Program was crucial to my success, so I was looking forward to sharing my back-to-work story. On top of the keynote, post-surgery I had my nutrition coaching clients, brand ambassadorships, other speaking engagements, acting work, and a potential contract job with Wellspect on the horizon.

In other words, I had a lot of shit going on. I knew I needed to become even more intentional and mentally strong before surgery. This is something I think isn't stressed enough in the medical community. The focus is on strengthening post-surgery through rehabilitation, nutrition, flexibility, etc. *What about pre-surgery?* For planned surgeries, it only stands to reason that the better shape you are in before surgery, the better the post-surgery outcomes will be. As someone who had been through many medical procedures, when I thought about going through yet another one, I felt an overwhelming sense of wanting to die. Now I had a choice: give in to the feelings of despair or face it head-on with a proactive approach. I thought to myself, *What better approach than 75 Hard?*

Bri, Nikki, and I decided to do it together. The Three Musketeers. All of us reached day 75 with no starting over and just in time for my surgery. No doubt being roommates helped us stay consistent. The day before surgery, I felt strong. I had a 14 percent increase in my endurance from day 1 to day 75. Back brace, broken spinal fusion, and all.

> It's overtime.
> All I keep thinking is to keep working until the buzzer.
> It's not over until it's over.
> Every minute is a moment to make progress toward my greater being, toward my success, toward my confidence, toward my debt to me.
> You are not my competition.
> You are my inspiration.
> Because I know if I can come from where you're at, YOU can come from where you're at.
> It's me vs me out here.
> And it's YOU who keeps me grinding.
> Head down, eyes up.
> I can't quit.
> I won't quit.
>
> —journal entry reflecting my pre-surgery mindset

My mom and Bri took me to surgery, which involved cutting my entire back wide open. I woke up after surgery in excruciating pain. I didn't remember it hurting that bad after the last surgery. While in the recovery room of the hospital, I began begging for pain meds. "Damn, my back hurts so bad. Please bring me pain meds and also bring my mom to me." Suffering that badly, I just wanted my mom. I saw my mom briefly, but the pain meds? "We need to wait until it's time to give you more pain medication." After I waited for what seemed like an eternity, they took me to a hospital room. I hurt so bad. My entire body. It felt like I'd been pummeled. When I was finally allowed to have pain meds, they dosed me up and I dozed off.

The most uncomfortable part of recovery, apart from the first 24 hours, was the itchy incision that ran down the length of my spine. That and the tight muscles in my neck and upper back. I was not able to wear a bra for weeks post-operation. Yet, the physical part of this revision surgery recovery period was a breeze compared to my first revision surgery. The only post-op medical complications I had to deal with were the discomfort of the sutures, a urinary tract infection (due to lack of movement and hydration), and anemia. It was only a few days before I was up and going. In fact, it was going so well I made it on that plane to Baltimore. The keynote speaking experience was everything I had hoped for and more.

23. Overtime

Before surgery, I had decided it was time to leave the orthodontic office to give myself transition time between surgery and my new contract position with Wellspect. It was not an easy saying goodbye because, at the time, I was getting along really well with a newly hired doctor. He treated me like his right-hand woman, the go-to person when something needed to be done. Over time, I developed relationships with my patients, many of whom were tagged as "Jesi-only" patients. They preferred me, and it felt so good to be preferred. Choking back tears, I said those goodbyes while sighing a massive sigh of relief. Once I recovered from surgery, it was time to start my new position.

My role was to introduce Wellspect products to the masses. A dream job but with a heavy, variable travel schedule. After two revision surgeries, you might think I'd have become weary of physical activity and travel, but it was just the opposite. I knew I wanted to continue my study of wellness and dedicate my life to helping others become the healthiest versions of themselves along the way. For me, Wellspect was part of that mission, so I left the orthodontist office and leaped toward this new opportunity. It was time to pursue my higher purpose while taking on a life mission of helping people by introducing clinicians to products that positively affect the quality of life for someone like me.

24

Believe

"Growing up, I had a toxic relationship with my body. After my spinal cord injury, it only amplified my hate for the skin I'm in. Every time I looked down at that massive para belly, I would become frustrated and upset with my circumstances. In reality, we must remember everyone has a belly when they sit. Here are some tips for controlling your appearance as a wheelchair user or able-bodied that may result in boosted confidence.

Go to the gym regularly. Over time your physique will improve, your energy will increase, your mental health will steady and you will s[l]eep like a rock. Be patient with the process. Take progress photos. Work hard.

Have regular bowel movements. A lot of that belly is bowel. I go at least once to twice a day.

Eat foods high in fiber to keep your bowels moving. Be sure to watch your caloric intake. As wheelchair users, we fail to realize we no longer need the standard 2200-calorie diet but we also need more than a restricted 1200-calorie diet.

DRINK WATER (unsweetened tea or black coffee). Avoid sugary and carbonated drinks. This will prevent weight gain and bloating.

Work on your appearance. Wear nice clothes, keep up with personal grooming, and focus on having a nice posture. People treat you according to how you carry yourself.

Every day, express 7–10 things you physically and emotionally love about yourself. It may be the same each day. Take a moment to be proud of the work you put in."

—social media post, eight years post-accident

24. Believe

As a kid, I used to do this thing where I'd make a wish when the clock hit 11:11, 1:11, 2:22, or any matching number combination. You'd think I would have wished for a dirt bike, ATV, Jeep, motorcycle, etc., but I didn't ... perhaps because I was pretty well set in that department. No, I wished to be influential. While watching shows on Disney Channel, specifically *Wizards of Waverly Place*, I would ask myself, *How the heck can I get on the TV like Selena Gomez?* I wanted to be a star. I wouldn't just think it or wish for it, I knew it. I looked up at the evening stars, those magical twinkling lights, and believed I would make a massive impact on the world.

Of course, back then, the vision was of my star self cruising around in a sports car, not in a wheelchair. God's plan for us is full of surprises. Before the accident, acting was far lost in my mind as a dream, not even a possibility. Yet, without consciously trying, the experiences I was gravitating towards as a wheelchair user put me in the spotlight. The clinical trial brought me national media attention, including television coverage, when I was still hospitalized. Social media posts became social media videos. Brand ambassadorships led to speaking engagements. From that point, giving acting a shot wasn't a big leap.

My first open audition was at the local Charlotte-based Evolution Talent Agency. Amber talked me into going to the audition with her: "What do you have to lose Jes?" Amber is one of those friends who continuously pushes you out of your comfort zone. She sees the potential in you before you see it yourself. She auditioned first. When she came out, she explained to me—a newbie, after all—what a slate was, how an actor verbally identifies themselves in an audition. "When you enter the audition room, you first give your slate, stating your name, location, and age," she schooled me. "Be sure to be loud and clear enough so they can hear it from a distance." A couple more individuals went, and then my name was called. I auditioned using a mock commercial script.

Afterward, I was offered an agency contract and invited to a three-week acting boot camp. *Holy freaking crap. I am agency represented talent.* For the first time in my life since getting injured, I started thinking everything would be okay. This was it. Life was about to change, I could feel it. And yet ... it didn't work out that way. I would go on to audition more than 100 times to get a handful of parts, including filming a new pilot for a show called *Date Me* and another called *Shop Girls*, along with a couple of bank commercials and a Walmart health commercial. Eventually, I got signed with Nomad Agency on the West Coast, which was very cool, helping me navigate modeling deals later on.

When I wasn't acting, there was so much more to do, and to some degree, everything required public speaking, influencer, and leadership skills. My social media platform was reaching numbers I found hard to believe. Every month, my calendar was filled with podcasts or speaking appearances. I was profiled in magazines like *New Mobility*, *Shape*, and *Woman's Day*. Life was busier than ever. To lighten my load, Bri became the new director of the Wheel With Me Foundation.

Eight years after my accident, I truly started believing in myself, and I think a large part of that feeling came from my friendship with Bri. She embodied this no-excuses, get-it-done attitude that allowed us to do much more together than we could alone. Believing in yourself sounds simple, but it's super hard work. My transition from angry victim to confident survivor took years, but the first step was the hardest. I had to let go of feeling sorry for myself.

One of my favorite old scripts to read over and over in my head was many variations of this:

It is so much harder for me to work, travel, save money, socialize, dress, shower, etc., compared to others because I am medical supply and wheelchair dependent in a world that doesn't always accommodate or care about me.

The mental dialogue I most loved to cling to also kept me in a perpetual state of feeling angry and defeated. If I wanted to feel better, my self-talk had to shift. Little by little, the voice in my head changed: *Life is not designed to be fair. Challenges make me stronger. Effort and attitude are the best weapons against any negative circumstance.*

Today I find that the more I help others and, in a real sense, truly live for others, the more I like who I am. Helping others is the best version of me. I'm truly becoming better. *Jesi may turn out to be an okay person after all. Jesi may have been paralyzed before her legs stopped working. Jesi May is finally free.*

In coaching, my number one priority is to help my clients see that they have the power to achieve whatever they want to achieve in their life. It's just a matter of how much effort they are willing to put in to make that happen. In the beginning, it's oh so much effort. At this stage, the critical talking point becomes that it's indeed hard at first, but little by little, the effort you need isn't minimal, but it will get easier. The intensity of the beginning stage is not permanent or linear for the rest of our lives. Once you believe in your ability to achieve the life you want, you can set goals and create a plan to make whatever you desire happen. You get out what you put in.

Of course, life can't be about working hard all the time. You have to play, too. Dating as a paralyzed woman was a bit scary for me. Especially blind date situations. I had this ridiculous fear that I was going to get taken into the sex trade. Despite what some people think in terms of the sexual desirability of a disabled woman, my disability makes me an easy target. So my fear wasn't baseless.

As soon as I told myself I was too afraid, a quiet internal dialogue presented a counterpoint: *Maybe I am ready to face those fears and find a long-term partner.* I met a few guys on dating apps and went on some dates—multiple dates, even—but nothing lasted. Once, a friend set me up, and it didn't work out. There were signs, though, that I was emotionally maturing when it came to physical restraint. On a first date with a hot guy from the Bumble dating app, I declined his invitation to come up to his apartment. That simple act, common sense to many, showed huge growth for me, since I usually gave in to temptation. It was time to give my body the respect it deserves.

I reconnected with a wheelchair user I'd met early in our injuries. Someone I thought had mature relationship potential. Remembering our past attraction and not trusting myself 100 percent, for our first get-together I brought Bri with me for that all-important voice of reason and to chaperone the situation. I wanted him in my life but didn't want to get sucked in emotionally only to have him ghost me. We parked; I got out and got to the front steps. There was no ramp. He never added a ramp to the front door of his place; he just bumps up the two steps, which tells you a bit about his personality.

As soon as he opened the door, I felt it. Thick sexual energy between us. We made pleasantries as I entered, but he never took his eyes off me. Instead, without saying a word, he maintained eye contact, embraced me, and went in for a passionate kiss. This gesture took my breath away. Every emotion I'd had for him years before came rushing back so strong. *This could be my person.* Cue the little heart bubbles in the cartoons popping around my being. Never mind my reservations because of the practical complexities of dating another wheelchair user. Five minutes in and I was a goner.

For the first time, I settled into a fully committed relationship, at least on my end. I wanted to do it right for once, and from the get-go, I was 100 percent honest. I said, "I'm not going to be your hook-up buddy. I want something serious." He responded, "I understand. To be honest, I wasn't looking to date anyone right now, but you are different because I don't want to miss my chance." It was hard at first to share myself with another person. Slowly, I began developing deep trust for him, myself, and the idea of love. Yet, he never actually gave me a reason to trust him. At least not in action, only in words.

This was so good; he opened my mind and body. I didn't realize I could feel or be as sexy as he showed me I was, especially in the bedroom. I didn't realize how much the spinal cord injury had robbed me of the joy of true connectedness with another human. He taught me how to use my body, move my body, and find pleasure in my body. He helped me find my sexuality, including confidence in myself. In a practical way, he was very knowledgeable about finances, saving money, and preparing for the worst. He helped me examine my finances to see where I could tighten up and make better financial choices to support my house purchase goal.

When we were together, it was great. Yet when we were apart, it felt like a long-distance relationship. Sparse communication and only pre-planned get-togethers. His actions made it clear he didn't want to allow someone fully into his life. My own emotional investment in what I thought he could be allowed me to ignore reality and keep pursuing him, ultimately setting myself up to be hurt. The physical connection clouded my vision as I told myself a lie: *Our relationship is perfect.* It took me a few months to notice his lack of communication. Next came judgment for paraplegic problems. Although he has a spinal cord injury, he never struggles with the typical bowel/bladder issues most of us do, resulting in him being impatient and judgy about it. Especially the fact that I wear a pull-up. I don't have urinary accidents often, but if I do, without a pull-up, any occasional incident will add a massive inconvenience to my day. So, I wear my child's pull-up for convenience and peace of mind.

His judgy commentary only amplified my existing self-consciousness. Plus, there was the lack of communication. He was slow to respond to my texts or voicemails. That safe feeling started to dissipate, like morning fog on a windshield. His face-to-face communication was immaculate. We had deep conversations, shared similar ideas of the world, and were honest. But, when we were apart, he was a mess when it came to managing his emotions and time. The relationship was feeling more and more one-sided.

Seven months into our relationship and a week before I left on the trip to Sweden, he sheepishly said, "I wish I could love you as you deserve." I should have known this was it. Déjà vu from my past, as I'd said those same words to The Nurse. Maybe this was my karmic due for how I had used men.

Gradually but with certainty, our communication became sparser. When I pushed for answers, I received a text saying he didn't have the time to start something new. *Seven months in, and he couldn't have thought to tell me that a little sooner?* At least he didn't completely ghost me. Regardless, I was crushed. My feelings had gotten in the way of reading the signs. I sobbed for a month, straight up heartbroken. I journaled a lot during that period, even listing my nonnegotiables and desires for a partner next time because once again I had compromised my values to be with someone. Letting go of the relationship, I made myself a promise. *I know my worth. I will never settle again.*

After the messy ending, Bri and I were driving to a nearby event, so we spontaneously stopped by my ex's condo to pick up my things. Fresh out of surgery and not ready to face him, I sent Bri, in the rain, to do my errand. After about five minutes, she came out victorious. He answered the door naked, saying, "Wish you had told me you were coming by. I would have loved to talk to Jesi and you." Of course he was naked. He was the definition of the cliché "some things never change."

I didn't feel like I got the proper closure, but since he didn't want me or only wanted me for sex, I knew I had to respect myself enough to keep my distance. When he reached out a year later to make plans, I considered it but let the booty call go, responding that I wasn't getting on his roller coaster again. *Fool me once, shame on you. Fool me twice, shame on me. I will not be fooled again.*

25

God's Plan

"The stone which the builders rejected has become the chief cornerstone."
—Psalm 118:22 New King James Version

As I write, I am nearing the tenth anniversary of my life-changing accident. My greatest lesson has been that nothing in life is permanent. Humans are in a constant state of change. The single thread running through anything productive I've done is change. Even the unproductive years involved change. From sassy, spoiled kid to fearless, reckless teenager to self-indulgent young adult. God's will changes you whether you participate or not. In recent years, change has meant staying open to trying new things, especially new ways to care for myself, my injuries, time management, relationships, sexuality, and my developing career.

In caring for myself, I continue to search for new ways to naturally heal my spinal column and improve my overall quality of life. It may not be sexy to talk about, but bowel and bladder management tops my list when it comes to quality of life. Wellspect introduced me to their LoFric catheters, which, combined with my lifestyle changes, ended my battle with chronic urinary tract infections. Freed from the infection cycle, I'm Wellspect's brand ambassador and number-one fan. After trying LoFric for a few years, I tried their bowel product Navina Smart for bowel management. Rather than having the weird chemicals and set times with suppositories, I simply use warm tap water that fills the rectum and lower intestine through a rectum catheter. It takes me 10 to 15 minutes to complete my full bowel program, with minimal booty-hole finger blasting. That's a win!

After bowel and bladder, I take care of my bones. Short on resources, I scoured the Facebook group Disability Trading Zone.

The Freedom Longevity & Wellness crew (back, from left: Tony, Ben, and Jamie).

On that page, I found an affordable used standing frame. This is different from the knee-ankle-foot orthotic leg braces for walking. It's a stationary device that holds you in a standing position. As I became stronger in my leg braces, I added ankle weights to my 45-minute workout. Other times I add a weight vest or lift a dumbbell in various ways to fire up my core.

Another natural technique for wellness I use is called brain tapping. My brain tap device uses refined binaural beats and isotonic tones to elicit neuron-plastic changes. To enhance the effectiveness, I wear a BrainTap headset to provide a third form of brain treatment: light therapy directed through the retinas and ear meridians. My calendar is blocked for a few minutes of brain-tapping in the morning. After tapping, I am much more centered and focused throughout the day. See https://braintap.com?afmc=2bi.

For my whole body, I schedule regular massages. This is my way of taking care of the parts of my body I don't have control over, to preserve them. After all, they are still a part of my body. I get regular massages. I also keep up with Pulsed Electromagnetic Field Therapy home treatments. The Pulse brand device distributes a low magnetic stimulation to help with my bone integrity, muscle stimulation, and joint pain. I've also found it helps with my spasms and nerve pain. I use wearable therapies to stimulate my muscles while helping with nerve pain, muscle mass, spasms, and circulation.

Cold water therapy is another way I build up my mind. I started this practice to prepare for Tough Mudders. I find ice baths the most effective, but cold showers also work. Yeah, it sucks in the beginning. Until it doesn't because the magic happens. You feel alive, really alive, confident, and energized. Doing this hard thing prepares you for other hard things. Cold water therapy builds confidence and stamina at the same time. It also provides a side benefit of reducing inflammation and muscle soreness, boosting cardiovascular performance.

I continue to use cannabis in the form of full-spectrum CBD called Recovery CBD for pain management and psychotropics a couple of times a year for mood improvement. I use THC only intermittently after realizing it was just another way to numb myself. I want to feel everything I can on my path to personal excellence.

I try to limit the amount of pharmaceuticals I put into my body. Food and exercise are my favorite medicines now. I traveled a long way from blindly taking the 10 prescription pills given to me following my accident. While there is a definite need for pharmaceuticals and many can be lifesaving, the more I studied, the more convinced I became that natural remedies, when possible, are better than manufactured ones. Even if they take a little more time and effort.

As I've begun to embody and gravitate toward holistic fitness in my daily life, I've connected with an increasing number of like-minded people. People I've met online, through 1st Phorm, CrossFit, the wheel community, Tough Mudder, and the off-road power sports industry. Without me forcing it or even consciously trying, an opportunity to pull together all that I have become—all that I am passionate about—into one business venture was proposed to me by an individual involved in those circles. This proposal happened because of a newly formed local business, Freedom Longevity & Wellness.

Through Instagram, they invited me to check out their space. I knew Freedom was close to where I lived and that they offered natural, holistic remedies for recovery and wellness, which sounded cool, but still, when the day came to check them out, I almost didn't go. I wanted to curl up with my dog Roxanne and hang out with Bri. Take a break from meeting new people. Then I thought, *A promise is a promise.* I sucked it up and went as scheduled to the two-hour appointment.

Going into Freedom Longevity & Wellness for the first time, I felt spirit wash over me. *This is my place, and these are my people.* I was scheduled for two hours but stayed for five. The conversation was incredible. The vibes were great. The facility itself is a neat space. I connected and got close to one of the owners especially, and we continued our conversation about mindset and business long after meeting. We talked about how Freedom didn't have a disability model but serves everyone regardless of age or ability. Eventually, after several weeks of conversation, I was invited to become a business partner. Freedom needed a third partner for two reasons. First, they weren't yet making expenses, and second, someone they trusted stole significant amounts of money not delivering on what was promised, setting them up for hardship before their doors even opened. A big lesson and reminder for us to be more cautious with background checks before going into business with others. I wasn't looking for a business opportunity, but if I'd learned anything since my accident, it was to be open to God's plan.

I was offered a 20 percent share. I responded, "I work a very inconsistent travel schedule. Is that a problem?" The owners reassured me that they'd make it work. Taking a leap of faith, I visited my disability navigator. "I know I have money set aside in my ABLE account. Could I use that to invest in the business?" They said, "Yes, absolutely you can." I thought, *Hell yeah, let's go!* In a matter of days, paperwork was signed and I was a proud partner. Although I knew I didn't need to add one more thing to my already full plate, I could feel God guiding me in this direction and, of course, I jumped in.

As a partner, I tasked myself with getting systems in place. I did this with the help of a business coach and a systems coach. I'm a big believer in the coaching model. Coaches help us grow to be the best version of ourselves. That's why I chose to be a nutrition coach and seek out coaches for myself. With systems in place, the business quickly moved out of the red and continued to gain momentum. We all learned together how to give our best and be our best. I got to roll what I'd learned and fought hard to become into one business model filled with like-minded customers. We talked about nutrition, personal challenges, and recovery goals.

Each day I work at Freedom, I wheel around our facility rotating between members in recovery stations. Sometimes I'm coaching someone through their first cold plunge or infrared sauna, or assisting a client into compression boots. Sometimes it's simply hugs or cups of water. Other times, I'm rotating through the stations myself, including VibeX, a whole-body vibration platform that uses a circular vibration pattern to recalibrate the central nervous system. It has proven to be a miracle in improving the touch and temperature sensation I lost so many years ago. I simply position myself on the plate while moving my legs through various positions. Based on my results, I love all of the recovery stations at Freedom, but the vibration plate has become one of my favorites (along with the cold plunge and Pulse electromagnetic fields mat).

Helping others fills me up like nothing else. When not working, I share experiences and insights on social media. As anyone influencing can tell you, being an internet personality makes you vulnerable. You are attacked as much as you are loved. Holding onto those wins keeps me going. This is a message from a longtime follower, a retired U.S. Air Force veteran who showed appreciation for my patriotism and did not sugarcoat the content: "Hi Jesi, I wanted you to know a third oral cancer came roaring into the base of the mouth. I started end-of-life hospice care this week to help with the pain. Please know how much I've enjoyed your posts. I'll be following you long after my Instagram stops."

In response, I decided to send a video back. Before I could get words out, I began crying. I felt so much sadness that his life was at its end. Tears and all, I hit record. "I am so sad to hear about your cancer but very grateful you took the time to let me know. May God hold you close and bring you into the light."

After sending the video, I prayed for the Lord to take him. I cried some more. I could not believe that this man, who had never met me, who only knew me through a screen, had taken the time to let me know that though his life was coming to an end, he would be an angel looking out for me.

We never realize the gravity of the impact we have on one another. This, my dear reader friends, is the power of community. To hold or pick each other up, lean on, and sometimes simply stand by. Of course, I didn't know any of this as a wild child tearing up the racetrack. Or those years of lying, cheating, and generally making a mess of my life. Look up no matter how far you've fallen, paralyzed or not. God has a plan for you. No one is too broken not to be 1 percent better the next day, a notion promoted by James Clear, author of the wildly popular book *Atomic Habits*. The life you want to live is on the other side of creating systems to allow you to achieve. Small changes in your routine to ultimately become the best version of yourself. Embodying what it means to be the change you want to see. Tasks completed while showing up first for yourself as your own life's hero and then showing up for others.

What I'm doing now is so much bigger than walking. Someday I hope to share my life with someone who wants to explore every corner life has to offer. If not with an individual, with a team of others focused on changing lives. I hope to have children of my own. If I don't, the individuals I impact will fill that void. I want to live my dreams, embracing the journey as much as possible, both the good and the bad. I accept where I am at this moment, knowing I will grow with each turning page of life.

All I ask for is strength to get through each day—strength from God, community, and that strong-willed baby in the toddler Jeep. Sometimes, my mind's eye reaches back in time to watch my younger self spin around and around like a wheel herself, making a mess of everything in her path. She pauses for a moment, catching her breath. I approach her, and we hug tightly with an unspoken understanding, slow to let go.

Jesi May, everything is going to be okay. Who needs to walk when you have wheels?

Index

Numbers in **_bold italics_** indicate pages with illustrations.

Index

www.ingramcontent.com/pod-product-compliance
Lightning Source LLC
Chambersburg PA
CBHW021143090426
42740CB00008B/911